An Informix-4GL Tutorial

Paul Mahler

Prentice Hall, Englewood Cliffs, New Jersey 07632

Library of Congress Cataloging-in-Publication Data

Mahler, Paul.
   An Informix-4GL tutorial / by Paul Mahler
     p.   cm.
   ISBN 0-13-464173-6
   1. Data base management. 2. Informix-4GL (Computer program)
  3. UNIX (Computer operating system)   I. Title.
QA76.9.D3M32 1990
005.74—dc20   89-39760
                                          CIP

Editorial/production supervision: *Karen Bernhaut*
Cover design: *Lundgren Graphics*
Manufacturing buyer: *Ray Sintel*

The publisher offers discounts on this book when ordered
in bulk quantities. For more information, write:

> Special Sales/College Marketing
> Prentice-Hall, Inc.
> College Technical and Reference Division
> Englewood Cliffs, NJ 07632

The author has made every effort to provide accurate and useful
information. Errors may exist, though, and this book is offered
without any guarantees.

Informix, Informix-4gl, Informix-Turbo, Ace and Perform are
registered trademarks of Informix Corporation. UNIX is a
trademark of AT&T.

Printed in the United States of America

10 9 8 7 6 5 4 3 2 1

ISBN   0-13-464173-6

Prentice-Hall International (UK) Limited, *London*
Prentice-Hall of Australia Pty. Limited, *Sydney*
Prentice-Hall Canada Inc., *Toronto*
Prentice-Hall Hispanoamericana, S.A., *Mexico*
Prentice-Hall of India Private Limited, *New Delhi*
Prentice-Hall of Japan, Inc., *Tokyo*
Simon & Schuster Asia Pte. Ltd., *Singapore*
Editora Prentice-Hall do Brasil, Ltda., *Rio de Janeiro*

For Kathy

Contents

Foreword

Paul has written a great book for people to get up to speed on Informix-4GL and the data management principles that surround it. For those interested in maximizing programming productivity, this is an important component in keeping startup time in learning 4GL to a minimum.

Programmer Productivity has been important since the first instruction register was loaded with ones and zeros. In the 1970's I saw the major barrier—poor development tools—between workers and an understanding of the information around them. There was a wide gap between what developers could do and what they should have been able to do.

High level languages like COBOL, Fortran, Basic, or C require a great deal of set up work to first create a program framework. As the substance of the application develops, this skeleton changes and work already done has to be changed or discarded.

Rapid prototyping tools were needed for building applications quickly and standalone screen generators and report writers started to appear. At Informix we produced some of the best—and still do.

But we listened to our customers ask for even more flexibility: "We need to update the database with calculated values while printing a report. Give us update facilities in the report writer." "The forms package gives us default menus to add, delete or update records in the database, but we want to put in our own commands like SHIP-BACKORDER or DELETE-ORDER."

Our users wanted all of the features of a "world class" language. Tools like form generators and report writers work with default behaviors. Our users wanted the special case handling available with procedural syntax including if-then-else statements, while loops, variable declarations and assignment, and subroutine calls with parameter passing.

As we moved into the 80's, developers were using report writers and screen generators to try and create entire applications. Developers reported ten-to-one programmer productivity when using these tools. They wanted to use them for the whole job, but could not.

We struggled with a paradox. How could we continue to achieve at least a ten-to-one increase in developer power and add flexibility? Will adding all of the statements of a higher level languages cause us to lose the productivity advantage?

We took another careful look at programmer productivity and created a fourth generation language, or 4GL. The secret power behind the standalone screen generator or report writer was syntax very specific to the task to be performed. SQL has a sort verb, the report writer has a page header clause, and a group total syntax, and so on. We concluded that this usage specific syntax was the power behind 4GLs, and not the absence of procedural syntax.

With this understanding, we could provide our users with the tools they wanted. They wanted the power of a non-procedural language and the flexibility of a third generation language. They were asking for more procedurality in standalone modules. What we gave them was a new world class language, with non-procedural magical chunks of syntax and procedural constructs woven into the syntax of a single new language. We took the best non-procedural syntax features from our menu system, forms package, report writer, and SQL database interface and interlaced them into a procedural syntax designed to be the first and best programming language ever designed specifically for building SQL database applications. The result was Informix-4GL.

As we go into the future, developers are continuing to legitimately ask for more productivity tools. We now hear "Give us report code module generators and default application types that can be modified." The Informix-4GL product has progressed since 1984 to include even more world class language tools like the interactive code management environment and a very sophisticated source code debugging system.

In the future, code generators and templates will continue to come from Informix and very good third party suppliers. Informix-4GL is progressing on its path of becoming the "dBase of bigger computers" or "the language for SQL database development."

We find as we get increasingly more powerful tools that the tools can meet both the end user requirements for ad hoc systems and the code generator requirements of the developer. For example, the upcoming report writer from Informix provides a "point and shoot" interactive interface. Users can create reports easily; developers can use the code generator commands to produce Informix-4GL programs.

As we continue to get more powerful tools for developers, we also get closer to the users needs. As we take user tools, like spreadsheets, and make them more powerful, we see that 4GL metaphors can have the same power in non-database applications. For example, the Hyperscript 4GL-like macro language of the WingZ spreadsheet can create an application with a windowed 4GL look.

As end user tools get more connected to databases and get more flexible, and as developers tools get more interactive and generate more code, the seam between end user tools and 4GL tools will vanish. I do not think this will make systems builders out of all users, but we will have more sophisticated systems built by users and developers together in a more dynamic process. Data management and office automation will merge to become "information management."

Some basic concepts will always remain because they exit in the nature of data and processes. Those basic concepts are personified in 4GL and in this book. To a large degree, to understand the basic data management concepts and processes and to understand Informix-4GL are the same thing. We succeeded in the design of the language to the degree that this is true.

Roger Sippl
Chariman
Informix Corporation

Preface

Informix-4GL lets you build relational database systems that solve business problems quickly and easily. This book will teach you how to use Informix-4GL to create database systems quickly and easily.

You can create order-entry, accounting, sales contact management, shop floor control, or inventory systems. Any business application can be quickly created with Informix-4GL.

I wrote the sample programs for this tutorial in a few days. Writing the samples from scratch with a language like C could have taken months. Even a C program written with commonly available packages like screen formatters and file management software would have taken considerably longer.

An Informix-4GL system can be easily moved from one computer to another. Informix-4GL runs on many machines from many different manufacturers. Informix-4GL is available for a wide variety of operating systems—Unix^{tm}, DOS and VMS, for example. An Informix-4GL system can be built on any one system to run on all these systems. Any system you build with Informix-4GL will run with any of the operating systems and all the different computers.

This tutorial will make it easy for you to learn Informix-4GL and create relational database systems. The tutorial starts with an introduction to relational database practice. After this introduction are a variety of examples. The examples present each of the major features of Informix-4GL. The examples demonstrate how to build a database, how to write a program to manipulate the database, how to present information on screen, and how to write reports.

Before learning Informix-4GL you should have some computer familiarity. I assume that you are familiar with your own operating environment, for example, UNIX^{tm}, DOS, or VMS. You should already know how to create and access files, and how to edit them. Experience with another programming language, like C, is not necessary but is helpful.

Acknowledgments

I would like to thank all the people who helped me write and finish this book. In particular I would like to thank Roger Sippl, Sally Goodyear, Jack Hairston, "Rock" Solomon, and Dennis Allison for all their kind support.

Paul Mahler
Solothurn, Switzerland
August 1988

1

An Overview of Relational Database Management

This chapter describes what a relational database management system is.

WHAT IS A DATABASE?

A database contains data about various entities. This data is held in files that are called tables. For example, let's look at an auto repair business. In the auto repair business, you might have three entities in your database, parts, projects and suppliers. (Please note that identifiers for data and programs will always typeset in courier type: like this.) These three entities are represented by three different sets of data in your auto repair database.

The database also contains information about the relationships between the entities. For example, the two entities, parts and suppliers, have a connecting relationship. Individual parts come from various suppliers. The following figure shows this relationship.

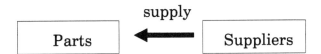

Suppliers could also supply parts for a specific project. This is a more complex three-way relationship between suppliers, parts and a third entity, projects. Projects have their own relationships to the other entities in the database. The following figure shows the relation between the three entities.

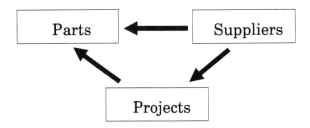

Relationships between entities are as much a part of the information about an enterprise as are data about entities. The relationships can be simple or complex. For this example, suppliers supply parts. This is a simple binary relationship where there are two entities with one relationship.

WHAT IS A RELATIONAL DATABASE MANAGEMENT SYSTEM?

A relational database management system is a computerized system used for managing the operational data of a business. It provides facilities for storing, accessing and modifying this data. A database management system provides facilities for

- Adding empty new tables to a database
- Removing tables from the database
- Accessing data held in the tables
- Sharing the data held in the tables
- Adding data to existing tables
- Deleting data from the tables
- Modifying data held in the tables

The following figure shows a simple database with two tables. The tables each contain data about my compact disk collection. There are two entities, CD (compact disks) and publishers. The relationship is that publishers publish CDs.

Music Database

cd

performer	cd_name	catalog
Talking Heads	Speaking in Tongues	2530154
Talking Heads	Little Creatures	253052
Talking Heads	Stop Making Sense	759925186
Waits, Tom	Frank's Wild Years	756790522
Wang Chung	Points on the Curve	4004-2

publishers

pub_name	performer
Geffen	Wang Chung
Island	Waits, Tom

The database management system allows me to create the two tables which will hold the information about CDs and publishers. It also provides me with tools to add to or delete information, or change the information stored about the two entities. It also provides tools for selecting parts of the data from either or both tables.

WHY USE A DATABASE SYSTEM?

Informix-4GL, an excellent example of a relational database system, provides commands for creating tables of information like the ones shown above. After you have created a table, you can add data to it. Informix also provides commands for removing data from a table or changing the contents of any record. It is also easy to delete multiple records, or add multiple records, or change multiple records with one operation.

You could write programs to manipulate the database. You could write programs to make a table, add data to a table, delete data from a table, or change the data in a table. You could even do all this with a text editor, as I did for the example above. Why use a database management system?

First, Informix Corporation has done all the programming for you. Instead of having to write a program to create a database, you can issue one Informix-4GL command. Rather than write a program to create a table, you can use a single Informix-4GL command. You can use single Informix-4GL commands to add data to a table, delete data from a table, or change the data held in a table.

Informix-4GL supplies a wide range of useful facilities. Even if you are able to duplicate many of them with programs you write yourself, you are not likely to duplicate all of them in any reasonable time. Do you really want to write your own programs to manage an audit trail of transactions for multiple concurrent users?

Second, Informix-4GL is likely to be more efficient than separate programs written from scratch. It uses sophisticated access methods to insure that operations are performed quickly. Because of this, adding to or changing a database is fast. Many man-years have gone into assuring the efficiency of Informix Corporation products.

Third, Informix-4GL is portable. An Informix-4GL application, written once, runs on small computers, big computers, and everything between. Informix-4GL is likely to run in all the environments you want your application to run in. You can write one Informix-4GL application and run it on many different computer systems.

Fourth, Informix-4GL gives you data independence. A program written to manage a specific file in a common programming language like C has to know a lot about the structure of that file.

If you change the program, you are likely to have to change the file. If you change the structure of the file, you will have to change the program. In the example, if you decide you would like the name of the album to come before the name of the artist, you will have to change the program everywhere it refers to the file.

With Informix-4GL the storage structure of data, or the method of data access, can be changed without having to change the programs that use this data. This gives you 4GL program immunity from any changes to the structure of your data.

Fifth Informix-4GL makes it easy to share data. Several users can use the same database. Informix-4GL already has dealt with the problems of concurrency control for you. This means if two or more people would like to get to a file at the same time, Informix-4GL will keep them sorted out for you.

Sixth, you can avoid data redundancy. (This is described at length in the following chapter on normalization.) A database system allows data to be shared between users and between applications. Data about an enterprise need only be stored in one location in order to be used by many different people for many different applications.

This means that data storage can be more compact. It also provides an opportunity to avoid some inconsistencies in the data and makes it easier to maintain the integrity of the data held in the database.

Seventh, you can reconcile conflicting requirements. A database holding information about many parts of an enterprise can be balanced against the needs of many users or applications.

Lastly, Informix-4GL provides other facilities past simple database management. These following sections describe the facilities, like the report writer and screen manager.

2
—

Relational Database Architecture

This chapter describes the architecture of a relational database system. If you are already familiar with the three architectural views of a relational database management system, you may want to skip this section.

THE THREE VIEWS OF A RELATIONAL DATABASE SYSTEM

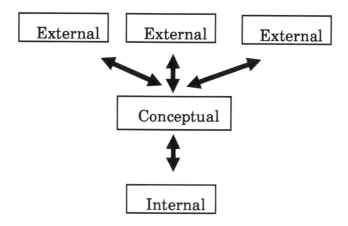

There are three possible views of a relational database management system, as shown in the figure above. Each of these views is described below.

From here on, the database management system in its entirety is called the DBMS. The DBMS includes all the parts of all three views of the database that are described below.

First, there is the internal view data storage and access. Second, there is the conceptual view of the entire database. Third, there are one or more external views of the database as seen by individual users.

The internal view shows how data is stored and accessed. The internal view deals with the physical structure and organization of data and the physical access to that data. With a database management system like Informix there is only one internal, or storage, view of a database for a given machine.

Informix manages these internal affairs for you. You do not really need to know how data is stored or accessed to be an effective Informix user.

The conceptual view of the database is a community view of the logical structure of an entire database. There is only one conceptual view of any individual database.

There may be one or more separate external views of a database for a variety of individual users. Each of these external views is how an individual user or programmer views the database. An external view represents one user's view of the database.

The following figure shows the music database again. I will use this example to help describe each of these three architectural views of a relational database management system.

Music Database

cd

performer	cd_name	catalog
Talking Heads	Speaking in Tongues	2530154
Talking Heads	Little Creatures	253052
Talking Heads	Stop Making Sense	759925186
Waits, Tom	Frank's Wild Years	756790522
Wang Chung	Points on the Curve	4004-2

publishers

pub_name	performer
Geffen	Wang Chung
Island	Waits, Tom

THE EXTERNAL VIEW

The individual user accesses the database through a language like COBOL, C, or Informix-4GL. The host language supports a variety of commands for accessing data held in the database. Each of these host languages has its own embedded data sublanguage and all users have their own external view of how to access the database.

ESQL is a data sublanguage for the C language. Here, Informix-supplied commands are added to the base C language. Any database manipulations are requested through ESQL commands which are used as additions to the C language.

Each data sublanguage includes a data definition language (DDL) and data manipulation language (DML.) The data definition language defines or describes database objects. The data manipulation language manipulates or processes these objects.

For example, SQL provides one set of commands for defining and creating the objects held in a database. It provides separate commands for accessing or manipulating these objects.

For the music database, a C programmer will have a different view of the database than a COBOL or SQL programmer. The user writing a C program to access the music database would view each data-record of the publishers table as a C data structure

```
struct publisher {
char publisher[18];
char performer[18]
};
```

A COBOL programmer would see each data-record as a COBOL record

```
01 PUBC.
02 PUB PIC X(18).
02 PERF PIC X(18).
```

Note the programmers have chosen different names for each of these structures. The C programmer has named the record pub-lisher. The COBOL programmer knows the record by the name PUBC.

THE CONCEPTUAL VIEW

The conceptual view represents the entire information content of the database. This view can be very different from the view of any individual user. The conceptual view represents the entirety of the data, not just a view forced on a user by the constraints of a particular language or type of computer.

The conceptual view of the database is defined in a conceptual view schema. From here on, we will just say schema to refer to the conceptual view schema. This schema includes the definitions of each table in the database and their constituent parts.

The data definition language used to describe the conceptual view is independent from the internal view of the database. The conceptual view of the database does not include how data is stored or accessed. The conceptual view does not deal with storage structures or access strategies. The schema describes only the information content and structure of the database.

As an example of the conceptual view please refer to the music database again. The music database contains information on two entities, CDs and publishers. The CD table contains information on each performer name, CD name and catalog number. Each data record in the publishers table contains a publisher name and an artist's name.

THE INTERNAL VIEW

Each data record in the CD table contains three data elements. The name of a performer, the name of the album, and a catalog number.

The performer name and album name are both strings of characters. Informix stores them as characters. This representation can vary from computer to computer.

For example, some computers may represent stored strings as a series of hexadecimal numbers. Other computers may represent them as a string of octal numbers. Each computer may also have its own method for specifying the length of a stored character string. Informix uses whatever storage representation is native to the target computer.

The catalog number is stored as a number since they do not contain any letters or punctuation in this example. Numbers are stored as different representations by different computers.

Informix uses whatever representation is appropriate for the computer at hand. This field might be stored as a 16-bit binary number on one computer, or as a 32-bit binary number on a different computer.

MORE ABOUT THE CONCEPTUAL AND INTERNAL VIEWS

The next figure shows a database manager, a file manager, and a disk manager. The database manager is the component of the database management system (DBMS) that administers the conceptual view schema.

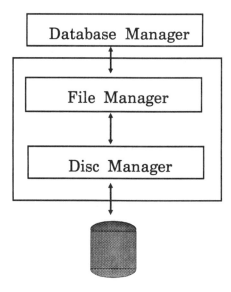

It is the database manager that supervises requests at the conceptual view level. It takes in requests and then issues the appropriate commands to the file management system to fulfill those requests. For example, the database manager can respond to requests to

- Access a named file
- Get certain data from a file
- Remove multiple records from a file
- Create a new file
- Remove an unwanted file

The the internal view has two components, a disk manager and a file manager. These two components taken together manage the internal view of the database. They are concerned with locating a specific item of data and presenting to the database manager. The methods for this access differ considerably from system to system.

Please note that while the names are very similar, the database manager is just a component of the database management system. Also, the database is the set of operational data administered by the DBMS. The database management system relies on the data manager to manipulate the database.

The internal view determines how an integer or string of characters is stored within a computer, or where this information is located. The internal view is also is concerned with the methods used by the database management system to retrieve information from memory quickly and efficiently.

The database is stored on some sort of physical media, usually a disk drive. This disk drive has its own logical layout. For example, it can be divided into a number of separate data tracks. The disk manager knows where information is stored physically on disk and the format it is stored in.

The disk manager performs all low-level physical input/output operations. It performs low-level operations like selecting a disk track and reading or writing data from this track. The disk manager is usually a component of the underlying operating system like UNIX or VMS or DOS. In some systems, like DOS or UNIX, this disk manager is called a driver.

The file manager regards the disk as a collection of stored files. The file manager takes in a request for a file, or a part of a file. It changes this request into commands understood by the disk manager in order to access the specified data.

For example, the file manager can process requests like:

- Get the first record from a named file
- Replace the second record in the named file
- Add a new record to a named file
- Create a new file
- Erase a named file
- Change the name of a file
- Move a file to a new location

The file manager does not need to know any of the details of the physical storage device. The disk manager isolates the file manager from the physical attributes of the storage device. It is the file manager that knows the name of this file and how to access it.

In many database systems, the file manager is also a component of the underlying operating system. It may, however, be replaced by the database management system's own file manager in the interests of increased performance. Informix-turbo, for example, provides its own file manager.

OTHER VIEWS

There are other views of the operational data of an enterprise than the views represented in the DBMS. These views may not involve files or data-elements at all.

There are other conceptual views of the data for a business or enterprise which deal in terms like entities and relationships that are not expressed in the database. Discussions of these modeling schemes are beyond the scope of this book.

3

Relational Database Structure

This chapter describes the structure of a relational database. Topics include domains, attributes, tuples, relations, normalization of a relation, keys, foreign keys and database integrity.

DOMAINS

The smallest unit of data in a relational database management system is a single data value like a catalog number or a name. These individual data items can be grouped together by type. For example, all the possible performer names that can appear in a database can be grouped together into a set. A set of all the possible values of a similar type is called a domain. For example, the domain of performer names.

The elements of a domain are all unique. Because of this, the elements of a domain are called atomic. There are no duplicate values in a domain. A domain is a mathematical set.

There may be more possible data elements in a domain than appear in a database. For example, there may be many more possible performer names than are in the database of compact disks that I own. The domain of data elements can be bigger than the number of data-elements that appear in the database.

In the compact disk database there are four domains of data: performer, cd_name, catalog, and pub_name. These domains contain all the possible values for a performer's name, a compact disk name, a catalog number, or publisher's name.

THE STRUCTURE OF A RELATION

The following figure shows the Music database again. In the relational database model, each table, for example the cd table, is called a relation. Now we will define exactly what a relation is.

Music Database

cd

performer	cd_name	catalog
Talking Heads	Speaking in Tongues	2530154
Talking Heads	Little Creatures	253052
Talking Heads	Stop Making Sense	759925186
Waits, Tom	Frank's Wild Years	756790522
Wang Chung	Points on the Curve	4004-2

publishers

pub_name	performer
Geffen	Wang Chung
Island	Waits, Tom
Warner	Talking Heads

First, a relation contains data from one or more domains. We say the relation exists *over* the domains. For example, the cd relation exists over three data domains, the domains of performer names, CD names, and catalog numbers. This is shown in the following figure.

A relation has two parts, a heading and *body*. This is shown in the next figure.

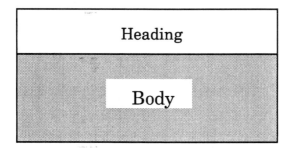

The heading of a relation consists of a fixed set of attributes. Each of these attributes heads a column of the relation. Each of the attributes is a name that corresponds to exactly one of the underlying domains. This is shown in the next illustration.

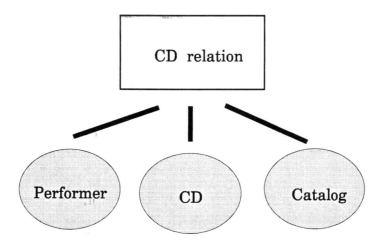

The number of attributes in the heading gives the degree of the relation. A relation with only one attribute in the header is unary. A relation with two attributes is binary and one with three *ternary*. Relations with more than three attributes in the header are n-ary, like 4-ary or 23-ary.

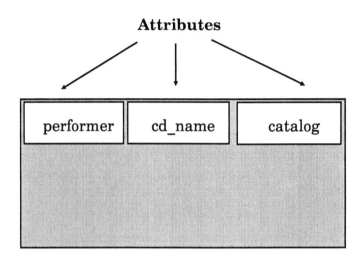

An attribute may be thought of as a name, or synonym, for the underlying domain. Separate relations can have different attributes that each exist over the same domain.

In the music database, for example, the performers and cd relations each have performer as an attribute in their heading. These attributes could have been performer in the performers relation and group in the publishers relation. In this case, performer and group would be synonyms and each relation would exist over the same underlying data domain of performer names. This is shown in the next figure.

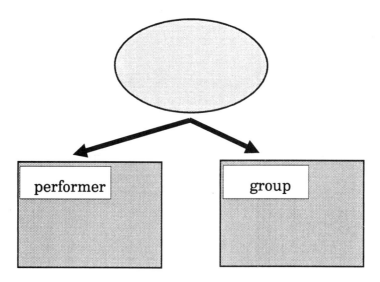

The different attributes of a single relation do not have to point to distinct underlying domains. More than one attribute of a single relation can exist over the same underlying domain.

For example, a sample relation could contain an attribute for a city where something originates and another attribute for a city that something is shipped to. In this case, the relation would have two different attributes, each of which would correspond to the same domain of city names.

If the same domain is used more than once in the same relation, the attributes must be different. Different names must be used in this case to distinguish the attributes. For example, for the two cities mentioned above, you might use `origin_City` and `destination_city`, instead of using `city` for both.

When using two different attributes that each exist over the same domain, you should use names that have two parts. A common part that names the underlying domain, and a distinct part that indicates the role of the unique attribute. In the cities case above, the data domain is `city_names`. The role of each attribute is destination or origin.

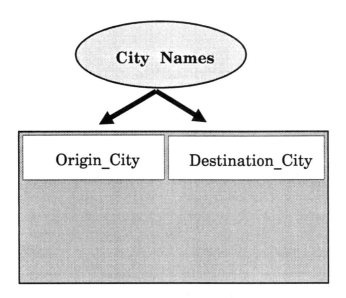

How can you identify attributes in separate relations with the same name? They may be qualified for unique identification. For example, the two relations `cd` and `publishers` each have a `performer` attribute. They can be qualified with the relation name to identify them as separate. One can be referred to as `publishers.performer`, the second can be identified as `cd.performer`. Note that the qualified name has two components, the relation name and attribute. The relation name and attribute are separated by a period.

The body of relation contains a set of *tuples* (which rhymes with couples). For example, the body of the `performers` relation as shown in the `music` database is a set of five tuples, one for each row shown in the figure. Each tuple contains an attribute-data pair for each attribute in the heading.

Relational terminology has a special name for the number of tuples in a relation. The number of tuples in the relation gives the cardinality of the relation. For example, the `performers` relation has a cardinality of five. A relation which has a heading, but contains no tuples has a cardinality of zero. A relationship with cardinality zero is called *empty*.

Each of the tuples in the example contains three pairs of attribute names and values. Here is an example of one tuple from the body of the Performers relation

```
{Performer,Wang Chung},
{CD_Name,Points on the Curve},
{Catalog,40042}.
```

In illustrating relations, the attributes are generally shown in the relation heading, but not in each tuple of the relation body. The body of the relation only shows the data element of each attribute-data pair. This is for ease of illustration only.

Relations are also usually illustrated as a table where each of the data values is shown in the same column. Each *column* of a relation contains an attribute which heads the column and is associated with one of the attribute-value pairs found in each tuple. Column is a loose term since there is really no left-to-right ordering of tuples within the body of a relation.

While the term column is often used in describing a relation, the data within a relation is not really held in columns. For example, the performers relation has three attributes in the heading: performer, cd_name, and catalog. One of the columns of the relation is the performer column. It contains the attribute performer found in the header and the {performer, data element} pair found in each of the five tuples in the relation.

As a database is used over time, the content of the database changes. Thus, the set of tuples in the body of a relation changes over time.

A database can contain one or more relations. The music database only has two relations. One relation contains information about individual compact disks. The other relation contains information about individual publishers. While this example only has two relations, a database can have many relations and usually does.

THE PROPERTIES OF A RELATION

The preceding section described the structure of a relation. It described each of the parts of a relation. There are other important properties of a relation. This section details some of these properties.

1. Relations may not contain duplicate tuples

The definition of a tuple comes from the mathematical theory of sets. The power of the relational model is in part due to this underlying model.

In the mathematical model of sets, no set may have duplicate elements. As a mathematical set, a relation cannot have duplicate tuples.

For example, the tuple

```
{performer,Wang Chung}{cd_name,Points on the
Curve}{catalog,40042}.
```

could only appear once in the Performers relation.

2. Attributes are unordered

There is no ordering to the attributes found in each tuple in the body of a relation.

For example, you should always refer to the `performer` attribute in the `music` database example rather than the second, or third, attribute of a tuple.

While a relation is often shown in figures neatly laid out in columns, it is important to note that there is really no ordering to the body of a relation. This is also why you can not really have a column of a relation. For example, these three tuples are equivalent:

```
{Performer,Wang Chung}{Disk Name,Points on the
Curve}{Catalog,40042}.
{Disk Name,Points on the Curve}{Performer,Wang
Chung}{Catalog,40042}.
{Catalog,40042}{Disk Name,Points on the Curve}{Per-
former,Wang Chung}.
```

3. Tuples are unordered

A mathematical set is unordered. As a set, the body of a relation is unordered. There is no top-to bottom ordering of the body of a relation. The tuples in the body of a relation can appear in any order. This ordering can also change over time as tuples are added or removed.

4. Attributes values are atomic

The underlying domains of a relation are simple. They are simple because they only contain atomic values. Because of this each of the data elements of an attribute-data element pair in a tuple is atomic.

This means that at any row-column position of a relation there is only one data value. Relations cannot contain repeating groups. For example, we could have listed the performers in our example database as

Disks

performer	cd_name	catalog
Talking Heads	Speaking in tongues	253052
	Little Creatures	253052
	Stop Making Sense	759925186
Waits, Tom	Frank's Wild Years	756790522
Wang Chung	Points on the Curve	40042

This is not a relation. It is not a relation because there are three sets of CD names and catalog numbers associated with the first performer name, *Talking Heads*.

NORMALIZING A RELATION

Any relation that satisfies property number four where all attribute values are atomic is called *normalized*. A normalized relation does not contain repeating groups of data. The process of turning an unnormalized table into a normalized relation is called normalization.

The process of turning an un-normalized database into a normalized database is also called normalization. The following chapter on logical database design addresses this separate issue.

We insist that relations be normalized because they are simpler that way. Because the relations are simpler structures, the operators used to work with them can be simpler.

For example, it is easier to insert a new tuple for a new *Talking Heads* CD into the cd relation than it is to change the table shown above. Inserting a new tuple for a new *Talking Heads* album into the normalized relation only involves the insertion of a new data-record. Inserting new information about a new *Talking Heads* CD into the table shown above requires adding new information to a set of information. This is because the normalized relation is a simpler structure than the unnormalized table.

WHAT IS A RELATIONAL DATABASE?

Now we can really tell you what a relational database is. A relational database is a collection of information that is seen by the user as a collection of normalized relations of various degrees where the set of tuples in any particular relation changes over time.

TERMINOLOGY

The parts of a relation are similar to more traditional data-processing terminology. A relation is like a *file*, a tuple is like a *record*, and an attribute is similar to a *field*. These are just similarities, however, and the relational model has a unique formal structure and nomenclature.

KEYS

Property one above says that a relation cannot have duplicate tuples. Since there are no duplicate tuples in a relation, it is always possible to have a unique key for any relation. The existence of a unique key makes it possible to find any individual record by using that key.

Some combination of the attributes of a relation can always be used to form a key which will uniquely identify any tuple in the relation. If no single attribute can be used as a key, a key can be made from several attributes taken together.

A candidate key is any unique identifier composed of one or more attributes that can be a key for a relation. By definition, every relation has to have at least one candidate key. This is because there is some combination of attributes which can be used that always matches only one of the unique tuples in a relation. Relations can have more than one candidate key.

The performers relation in the music database has two candidate keys. Since each CD has a unique catalog number, catalog is a candidate key. If each disk has a unique title, cd-name is also candidate key.

As tuples in a relation must be unique, the values of a key must address a unique tuple. No unique value for a key can address more than on tuple of a relation. For example, `performer` is not a candidate key to the `cd` relation because a single performer name does not always uniquely identify a single tuple.

Keys must also be minimal. A key constructed from a combination of the `performer` attribute and the `cd_name` attribute would be unique. It would uniquely identify any individual tuple. It would not minimal because you can drop one of the attributes and still have a candidate key. You could drop the `performer` attribute and still have `cd_name` as a candidate key.

It is possible for a relation to have more than one candidate key. When there is more than one candidate key, one of them is selected to be the primary key. Any other remaining candidate keys are then secondary keys. For example, we could pick `cd-name` as the primary key which would leave `catalog` as a secondary key. In use, relations often have just one candidate key. This example assumes that `name` is a unique identifier, that is there are no duplicate names.

Keys provide the only addressing mechanism that is available in the relational model. The only way to find a particular tuple in a relation is by knowing the name of the relation and the value of the key that addresses the desired tuple. The only way to find a particular tuple in a relation is by knowing the value of a key.

FOREIGN KEYS

No explicit relationship is shown between the two relations in the music database. There are no explicit links between relations in a relational database. The glue that holds a relational database together is keys. It is keys that allow one relation to be associated with another relation. It is the keys that allow connections to be made between data in one relation and data in another relation.

A selected attribute in one relation can be used to reference a primary key in another relation. An attribute in one relation that is used as a link to a primary key in another different relation is called a *foreign key*. It is a foreign-key because it is found as an attribute in this relation, but used to key into the other relation.

It is these foreign key to primary key matches which represent the references between relations. It is the foreign key to primary key references that link a relational database together.

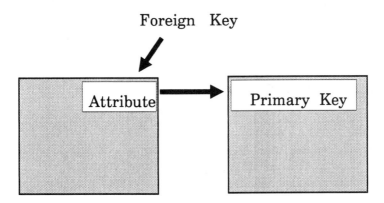

For example, each tuple in the cd relation contains a performer attribute. The performer attribute can be used as a primary key for the publishers relation.

Each tuple of the cd relation also contains a performer attribute. The performer attribute in the cd relation can be used as a foreign key.

The foreign key in the cd relation can be used to link to the primary key of the publishers relation. For example, by knowing that the value of the foreign key is Wang Chung it is possible to find that the publisher is Geffen.

Each performer in the music database has only one publisher. If a performer had more than one publisher, then `performer` would not be unique in the `publishers` relation and the `performer` attribute could not be a candidate key in the `publishers` relation or a foreign key in the `cd` relation.

The `performer` attribute is not a candidate key for the `cd` relation. There is no requirement for a foreign key to be part of the primary key of its containing relation. The foreign key does not have to be a candidate key in its containing relation either.

Lastly, a foreign key can be used to reference its containing relation. There is no requirement that a foreign key be used to reference only the primary key of separate, different, relations.

NULL VALUES IN A TABLE

A good relational database system, like Informix-4GL, provides a separate value when no data has been entered into a table. This is the `null` value. A specific value of `null` is entered into a table when there is no data available that the user has placed into the table. The user may also place `null` values into a table to indicate that no data is available.

TWO INTEGRITY RULES

There are two integrity rules in the relational model.

1. Entity Integrity

Attributes that are part of a primary key can not accept null values.

The primary key must satisfy the property of uniqueness. If one of the attributes of a primary key were allowed to be null, the primary key could no longer be guaranteed to be unique.

2. Referential Integrity

The value of a foreign key must be found as a value of the primary key in the matching relation, or the foreign key must be null.

For example, if the value of the foreign key performer is Wang Chung, then there has to be a tuple in the publishers relation where the data associated with the performer attribute is Wang Chung.

Unlike primary keys, foreign keys can contain null values. There doesn't have to be a primary key to foreign key match if the foreign key is null.

4
——

Operations on Relations

This chapter describes the operations that can be performed on a relation. Even if you are already familiar with selections, projections, joins and outer joins, you may wish to read this chapter. You will need to be familiar with each of these operations in order to use Informix-4GL successfully.

The operations that can be performed on relations are

- Selection
- Projection
- Union
- Intersection
- Difference
- Join

The theory of each of these operations is explained in the following sections of this chapter. Later chapters describe how to perform each operation with Informix-4GL.

Each relational operation results in a new relation. The first two operations, selection and projection, operate on a single relation to produce a third, different, relation. The remaining operations work with two relations and produce a third new relation.

SELECTION

You may select various tuples from a relation to produce a new relation. These selections can be based on the contents of the relation. For example, refer to the music database again. You could select each tuple from the cd relation where the performer is Talking Heads. This would select three tuples from the relation and create a new relation. This new relation would have three tuples. This relation would look like this:

New

performer	cd_name	catalog
Talking Heads	Speaking in tongues	253052
Talking Heads	Little Creatures	253052
Talking Heads	Stop Making Sense	759925186

You could select all the tuples where the catalog number is greater than 41000 but less than 260000. This would create a new relation with only two tuples

New

performer	cd_name	catalog
Talking Heads	Speaking in tongues	253052
Talking Heads	Little Creatures	253052

PROJECTION

Selection takes horizontal slices out of a relation. *Projection* takes vertical slices. Projection selects one or more attributes of a relation. For example, you could project just the `performer` and `cd_name` columns from the `cd` relation.

New

performer	cd_name
Talking Heads	Speaking in tongues
Talking Heads	Little Creatures
Talking Heads	Stop Making Sense
Waits, Tom	Frank's Wild Years
Wang Chung	Points on the Curve

Projection allows you to take just some of the attributes of a relation. Projection can also reorder the way that attributes appear in the header of the new relation. For example, A projection of `cd_name` and `performer` from the `cd` relation would produce a new relation that looks like this

New

cd_name	performer
Speaking in tongues	Talking Heads
Little Creatures	Talking Heads
Stop Making Sense	Talking Heads
Frank's Wild Years	Waits, Tom
Wang Chung	Points on the Curve

UNION

Union is the first operation that takes two relations and produces a third, different, relation.

A *union* is an operation from the mathematical theory of sets. In a mathematical union, the elements of one set are combined with the members of another set to produce a third set. This third set contains all the elements found in both the original sets.

In the relational model, the union operation combines the tuples of one relation with the tuples of another relation to produce a third, new, relation.

In order for two relations to be combined in a union, they must be union compatible. Three conditions must exist for two relations to be union-compatible. Here are the rules, followed by some examples.

First each relation must be of the same degree. If one relation has three attributes, so must the other.

Second, the attributes found in the heading of each relation must be each based on the same underlying domains.

Third, attributes in each relation that are based on the same underlying domain must appear in the same order in each relation heading. The equivalent attributes in the heading of one relation must be found in the same order as the attributes in the heading of the second relation.

These rules insure that the result of any union operation is still a relation. Without these rules, a union operation could produce a set without producing a relation.

Here is an example. Suppose we add a new relation to the music database which contains data about some of my classical CDs. (Well, these are classics to me, anyway.) The relation name is classical_cd. It has the same attributes as the cd relation:

New

```
        classical_cd
performer           cd_name              catalog
Mama's and Papa's   Greatest Hits        354234
Rolling Stones      Beggar's Banquet     2898232
```

The union of the `classical_cd` relation with the `cd` relation would produce a new relation containing all the tuples from both relations:

New

performer	cd_name	catalog
Mama's and Papa's	Greatest Hits	354234
Rolling Stones	Beggar's Banquet	2898232
Talking Heads	Speaking in tongues	253052
Talking Heads	Little Creatures	253052
Talking Heads	Stop Making Sense	759925186
Waits, Tom	Frank's Wild Years	756790522
Wang Chung	Points on the Curve	40042

The union operation is associative. This means that unions can be done in any order and will still produce the same result. For example, (A union B) union C is the same as A union (B union C).

INTERSECTION

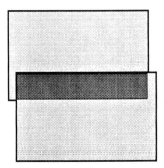

An intersection can only be performed on two union compatible relations. This operation also comes from the theory of mathematical sets.

The intersection of two sets contains only those elements that appear in both sets. The intersection of two relations contains only those tuples which are found in both relations.

For example, if my *Tom Waits* CD becomes a classic, I could make an entry for it in the `classical_cd` relation. Then the intersection of the `classical_cd` relation and the `cd` relation would contain only one tuple, the Tom Waits tuple. This is because only the Tom Waits tuple would be in both relations. This is shown in the following figure

New

performer	cd_name	catalog
Waits, Tom	Frank's Wild Years	756790522

DIFFERENCE

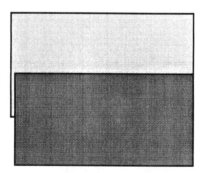

The difference operation can be performed on any two union-compatible relations. The difference of two relations contains all the elements of one relation that aren't found in the other relation.

The difference removes all the tuples from the first relation that can also be found in the second relation. Let's use the same Tom Waits tuple again for an example. If we have a Tom Waits tuple in the `classical-cd` relation then the operation:

```
cd minus classical_cd
```

would produce a new relation that had every tuple from the CD relation except the Tom Waits tuple

New

performer	cd_name	catalog
Talking Heads	Speaking in tongues	253052
Talking Heads	Little Creatures	253052
Talking Heads	Stop Making Sense	759925186
Wang Chung	Points on the Curve	40042

JOIN

Two relations may be combined with the join operation. The join combines, wherever possible, each tuple in one relation with one or more tuples from a second relation.

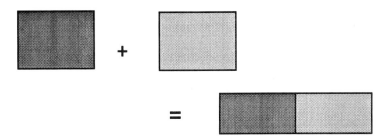

The first example joins `cd` to `publishers` where there is a match between publisher names. This join could be written as:

```
cd join publishers
```

Where `cd.performer` exists over the same domain as `publishers.performer`.

Note that the `performer` attribute is qualified in the selection statement above. This is to avoid confusing the `performer` attribute from the `publishers` relation with the `performer` attribute from the `cd` relation.

In Informix-4GL, the join is performed with the select statement. The select statement is described in detail in a later chapter. Don't worry about the syntax of the Informix-4GL select statement yet. This example is just here to help describe the join operation. It is not intended to teach you how to use the select statement. The chapter on the select statement will explain its use.

The join shown above would be written like this in Informix-4GL,

```
select all
from cd, publishers
where cd.performer = publishers.performer
```

This join would result in a new relation with the following attributes:

```
performer   cd_name   catalog   pub_name   performer
```

This example joins each tuple found in the `cd` relation to a matching tuple from the `publishers` relation. The tuples are joined through matching the specified foreign key with the specified primary key; cd.performer is the foreign key specified in the join and `publishers.performer` is the primary key.

Each tuple in the `cd` relation is taken one at a time. As each tuple is taken in turn from the `cd` relation, cd.`performer` is used as a foreign key to attempt to find a matching tuple in the `publishers` relation.

Wherever a match is found, the combined information is used to form a tuple in the new relation. Each new tuple contains all the attributes from each of the original relations disks and publishers. That is, each new tuple contains all the attributes from the cd relation and all the attributes from the publishers relation.

Only tuples taken from cd which have a matching tuple in the publishers relation would appear in the new relation. For example we can put another tuple into the cd relation. This tuple would not have a corresponding tuple in the publishers relation:

```
Rondstat,Linda Round Midnight   Asylum   60489-2
```

This is because there is no publisher named *Asylum* in the publishers relation. No tuple for Linda Rondstat would appear in the new relation for the join. Rondstadt,Linda, the foreign key found in the cd relation, would not match any primary key in the publishers relation.

The foreign key for this tuple, Asylum, would not be found in the primary key of the publishers relation. Such a tuple would, of course, violate the rules of relational integrity and should not be allowed in the music database.

In the above example, the same attribute, performer, appears twice. It appears once in each tuple selected from the cd relation. It appears again with each tuple selected from the publishers relation. If one of these two appearances is dropped it is called a natural join. The natural join would result in a relation like the following.

New

performer	cd_name	catalog	Name
Talking Heads	Speaking in tongues	253052	Warner
Talking Heads	Little Creatures	253052	Warner
Talking Heads	Stop Making Sense	759925186	Warner
Waits, Tom	Frank's Wild Years	756790522	Island
Wang Chung	Points on the Curve	40042	Geffen

Here is a second example of a join

```
select all
from publishers, cd
where publishers.performer = cd.performer.
```

Here, each of the tuples from the `publishers` relation is taken one at a time. Each is matched with any corresponding tuple in the `cd` relation by matching keys. This is what the resulting relation would look like:

New

name	performer	performer	cd_name	catalog
Geffen	Wang Chung	Wang Chung	Points on the Curve	40042
Island	Waits,Tom	Waits,Tom	Frank's Wild Years	756790522
Warner	Talking Heads	Talking Heads	Speaking in tongues	253052
Warner	Talking Heads	Talking Heads	Little Creatures	253052
Warner	Talking Heads	Talking Heads	Stop Making Sense	759925186

Note that the `Warner` tuple in the `publishers` relation matches several tuples in the `cd` relation. Wherever the foreign key `publishers.publisher` matches the primary key `cd.publisher` a tuple is created in the new relation. There must be a match between the foreign key and the primary key for a tuple to appear in the new relation.

There might also be extra tuples in the publishers relation which would not match tuples found in the cd relation. For example if we added this tuple to the publishers relation:

```
Decca   Moody Blues
```

Information from this tuple would not appear in the new relation formed by the example join. That is because the publisher *Decca* doesn't appear in any tuple in the CD relation. This extra tuple would also violate the relational integrity of the database.

SELECTION ON JOINS

In the example above, the join is restricted to tuples where performer names are the same in both relations, as in the selection

```
cd.performer = publishers.performer
```

Only tuples in the cd and publishers relation which can be linked with the selection criteria are used to form tuples in the new relation.

In the example above, the selection is based on equality between the foreign key and primary key. When the selection looks for equality between the two keys, the join is called an *equi-join*.

It is possible to make selections in many different ways. For example, selections can be made on inequalities. All the possibilities are discussed in the later chapter on the select statement.

The selection can also use attributes from either relation that are not in the primary key or foreign key. This example shows a join based on an inequality that uses a selection attribute that does not appear in the foreign key or primary key

```
select all
from publishers,cd
where publishers.performer = cd.performer
   and name is not "Geffen"
```

The relation resulting from this join would look like this

name	performer	performer	cd_namd	catalog
Island	Waits, Tom	Waits, Tom	Frank's Wild Years	756790522
Warner	Talking Heads	Talking Heads	Speaking in Tongues	253052
Warner	Talking Heads	Talking Heads	Little Creatures	253052
Warner	Talking Heads	Talking Heads	Stop Making Sense	759925186

PROJECTION ON JOINS

The results of a join can be restricted to certain attributes. For example, the natural-join is a projection of the equi-join operation. In the natural join, the equi-join is projected so that the foreign key or primary key only appears once in the new relation. Since the foreign key and primary key attribute are the same, the performer attribute only appears once in the new relation.

Other projections can be specified in the join operation. For example:

```
select performers.performer,performers.cd_name,
publishers.name
   from cd, publishers
   where cd.performer = publishers.performer.
```

This join and projection would produce the following relation which only has the performer, cd_name and name attributes

New

performer	cd_name	name
Talking Heads	Speaking in tongues	Warner
Talking Heads	Little Creatures	Warner
Talking Heads	Stop Making Sense	Warner
Waits, Tom	Frank's Wild Years	Island
Wang Chung	Points on the Curve	Wang Chung

EXTENDED JOIN

The result of a join is a new relation. This relation can then be used in a second join. It is possible to join several relations together in this fashion in an extended join. For example you could join three relations, a, b, and c together with a statement like

```
select all from a, b, c where . . .
```

This statement would first join a to b to form a new relation. This new relation would then be joined to c to form another new relation.

OUTER JOIN

In the outer join, the attributes of every tuple in the relation that contains the foreign key appear in the new relation. Each tuple from the relation containing the foreign key will appear in the new relation, even if there is no matching tuple in the relation containing the primary key. If there is no matching primary key, the attributes in the new relation that come from the relation containing the primary key are left empty.

All the joins described in the preceding sections were inner-joins. In an inner-join, there must be a match between the foreign key and the primary key for a tuple to appear in the new relation. This is not the case for the outer join.

Here is the `publishers` relation again with a new tuple added for the publisher *Decca*:

publishers

name	performer
Decca	Moody Blues
Geffen	Wang Chung
Island	Waits, Tom
Warner	Talking Heads

Here is an example of an outer-join:

```
select all
from publishers, outer cd
where publishers.performer = cd.performer
```

There is no tuple in the `cd` relation that corresponds to the publisher *Decca*. There is no primary key in the `cd` relation for the foreign key *Decca*.

In this outer join, the attributes from every tuple in the `publishers` relation is found in the new relation. The *Decca* tuple appears in the new relation, even though the foreign key *Decca* doesn't match any primary key in the `cd` relation.

Note in this example that there is a tuple for *Decca* in the new relation, but that there are no values for the attributes which would come from a corresponding `performer` tuple. The tuple from the `publishers` relation is concatenated with an all null tuple to make the tuple in the new relation. Any missing data is simply missing in the new relation:

New

name	performer	performer	cd_name	
Geffen	Wang Chung	Wang Chung	Points on the Curve	40042
Island	Waits, Tom	Waits, Tom	Frank's Wild Years	756790522
Warner	Talking Heads	Talking Heads	Speaking in Tongues	253052
Warner	Talking Heads	Talking Heads	Little Creatures	253052
Warner	Talking Heads	Talking Heads	Stop Making Sense	759925186

The outer join is very useful in real-world databases. Unlike other less powerful database management systems, Informix-4GL provides for outer joins.

SELECTIONS ON AN OUTER JOIN

Informix-4GL does not allow selections to be performed for an outer-join where the selection is based on any attribute not in the relation containing the primary key. For example, in the join used above

```
select cd.performer, cd_name, catalog, name
   from cd, outer publishers
   where cd.publisher = publishers.publisher.
```

no selections could be made on attributes in the publishers relation. For example, you can't select publisher.publisher = Geffen as shown in the following example.

```
select performer, cd_name, catalog, name
   from cd, outer publishers
   where cd.publisher = publishers.publisher
       and publishers.publisher = Geffen
```

5

Indexing and Accessing a Database

The information in this chapter will help you construct databases that will perform well. Topics in this chapter include indexing strategies and B-trees. The chapter describes what indexes are and when to use them. The 4GL statements that you use to build and remove indexes are described in chapter 10.

DATABASE PERFORMANCE

Data for a DBMS is held on some sort of physical device. This could be a disk drive, a floppy disk drive, or an optical disk drive. These various storage devices are used instead of main memory because they are cheaper. It is much less expensive to hold a million characters of data on a floppy disk than in main memory.

Disk drives are slower, not just cheaper. Accessing a byte of data in main memory can be thousands of times faster than accessing the same data from a floppy disk.

A good DBMS minimizes the bottleneck of disk access. Minimizing disk access time maximizes DBMS speed. This chapter describes how data can be stored so that it can be accessed as quickly as possible.

The storage structure of a file is the physical arrangement of data on a given device. The selection of a storage structure is called physical database design.

The physical database design determines database performance. A good physical database design will provide for fast applications.

The database designer needs to determine how the database will be used. You must know what applications will use the database, how often they will be run, and how they access data. This chapter will help make good physical database design easier.

INDEXING

Database access can be speeded with the use of an *index*. A database index works like the index in a book.

A book index is a list of key information about various subjects held in alphabetical order. If you are looking for information about a certain topic, you can look in the index. You run down the list of topics searching for the one that interests you until you find the right key.

Next to the key in the index is a page number. You can use this page number to find the section, or sections, containing the data you are interested in reading. Having the index item and the page number is faster. Once you find the key item in the index, you can go right to the data you are interested in. By searching the index, you do not have to search the whole, much larger, book. The key takes you right to the page you want.

You could find the information you are interested in by thumbing through the book a page at a time, or by looking at pages at random. This would be slow.

SORTING BY INDEXING

The index can also be used for sorting information. Information can be selected from the book in sorted order by selecting each data item one at a time in the order found in the index.

There is some overhead associated with this index. First, someone had to compile the index. This took time. Second, the index takes up some extra space.

An index is a space-time trade-off. By allocating space to the index, you are reducing the amount of time needed to search for data. By taking the time once to compile the index, you are reducing the amount of time needed every time you search for something.

A database uses indexes like a book index. Although building the index takes time and space, having it speeds data retrieval.

The next figure shows how an index can be built for the Performers relation in the Music database. In this example, there is an index to the left of the Performers relation. This index is sometimes referred to as an inverted list.

The inverted list is an index of performer names. You can use a performer's name to look in the index. Having found the performers name in the index, you can quickly find each record for that performer in the performers relation.

This is, of course, a trivial example. This index really isn't saving you much time. It would be just as fast to look through all the records in the Performers relation for *Talking Heads* albums.

This changes dramatically as the relation gets bigger. As the relation gets bigger, it becomes faster to use the index, and slower to search through all the tuples. The index slows down any updates to the database. Whenever the datbase is changed, the index must be changed, too.

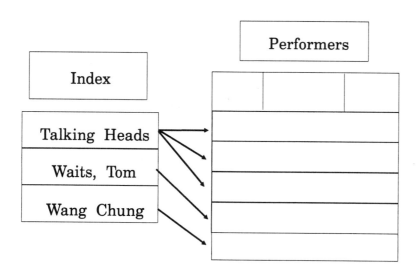

WHEN AN INDEX SHOULD BE USED

There is an easy practical test to determine when you should add indexes to a database. If your application is running slowly when it looks for data in the database, you should consider building an index. If it takes more than a few seconds to get data back from a database search request, you probably need an index.

You should build an index whenever you need to search a relation frequently for the same attributes. For example, if your application searches the performers relation frequently for album names, build an index for the cd_names attribute. Building the index is fast and easy and can dramatically speed the access to data held in the relation.

Chapter 10 describes Informix-4GL statements that are used in managing indexes and gives examples of their use.

WHEN AN INDEX SHOULD NOT BE USED

In the example above for the music database, the index on the performers relation didn't help much. It was easier to search the small performers relation for an album name than to search the index.

You should not build an index on any relation that contains less than a few hundred records. The index won't help, in fact it will slow you down.

OVERHEAD FOR AN INDEX

The index for a data-element can take nearly as much storage space as the data being indexed. Typically, half as much space is devoted to an index as to the data it is indexing. If you have a music database of your own with 100,000 bytes of information stored about performers, an index to performers might take 50,000 bytes.

It is also typical to have half the total storage requirements of a database devoted to indexing. Indexes can take as much space as data. For example, if you have a database that contains 10MB of data, you might use another 5MB for indexing.

MULTIPLE COLUMN KEYS

Informix allows a single index to be built on more than one column at the same time. For example, you could build an index on a key made from the performer and album attributes in the cd relation. This is called a *multiple-column index or composite* index.

The multiple-column index is not restricted to candidate keys. In many cases, access to the database can be improved with a multiple-column index.

B-TREES

This section describes very briefly the internal structure Informix-4GL uses to build index. Informix-4GL uses B-trees.

This section may be skipped if you are not interested in B-trees. You can use Informix-4GL without knowing what a B-tree is. For a full discussion of B-trees, you may read *The Art of Computer Programming* by Donald Knuth.

You build an index to a relation so that the index can be searched instead of the relation. An index is searched so that the larger unordered relation does not have to be searched.

The index must still be searched, though. If the index is very large, searching the index can take a lot of time. The index can be searched faster if we build another index, an index to the index. This scheme of indexing the index is called *multi-level indexing* or *tree-structured indexing*.

Many levels of indexes to indexes can be constructed. In practice it is rare to have more than three levels of indexing.

There are various indexing methods available for data stored within a computer. There is no one best storage structure for all types of indexes. The best index depends on the application. In general for most business applications, B-Trees work very well. Informix-4GL uses B-Trees. A B-Tree is a particular sort of multi-level or tree-structured index.

With B-Trees, the tree-structured index is constantly updated to stay "in balance." The B-Tree is updated with every change to the index so that it automatically stays in balance.

A B-tree minimizes the distance from the beginning of the index tree-structure to any specific index item. Balancing the tree-structure minimizes the time needed to access any individual item in the index.

6

Logical Database Design

How should a schema be organized? What relations should be in a database? What attributes should go in a relation? Why should an attribute go in one relation instead of another? These are questions about logical database design.

It is beyond this book to give an in-depth tutorial of logical database design or database design methodologies. This chapter will only introduce some of the issues of logical database design.

Logical database design has two important parts.

First, a good logical database design produces a schema that accurately represents the structure of the real-world data that will be put in the database.

The data about any enterprise has its own natural logical organization. Part of database design is building this natural design into a schema.

Second, a good logical database design should lessen redundant data. Redundant data makes a database more difficult to update or change. A logical design which reduces data redundancy will provide improved performance. This chapter shows various guidelines for organizing a database to reduce redundant data.

NORMAL FORMS

It is better to have simple relations and a simple schema. In simple relations nonkey attributes only contain information directly related to the primary key.

It is undesirable to have nonkey items in a relation that are not logically associated with the primary key. There are rules that have been developed to help you verify that relations do not have this undesirable property. These rules are expressed as *normal forms* which are described below. There are a series of constraints that a relation must fit to be in a certain normal form.

Normal forms, as described in the following sections, are guidelines for the organization of a schema. The normal forms help you tell when relations are not well organized. A relation that is in one of these normal forms is called *normalized*. A schema where the relations are in normal forms is also called *normalized*.

There are also simple methods, described below, for changing a relation that is not normalized to a relation that is normalized. Normalization is the process of changing an unnormalized relation to a normalized relation.

Let's start with a simple example of what a normalized relation looks like.

A relation must, by definition, have a primary key. The normal forms are just a way of expressing the common-sense notion that all the other attributes in a relation should only contain information that is directly about the primary key.

For example, look at the following simple relation which has two attributes, name and extension. There is only one candidate key in this relation, name. The structure of the data is simple. Each individual uses a certain phone and users may share a phone.

```
name       extension

Paul          10

Susan         10

George        14

Sabrina       16

Bill          18

Karen         20
```

This relation of the extension to the name can be shown in a simple diagram. The diagram shows that the extension number depends on the name of the person; that is each person has their own extension

This is a normalized relation because the information in the nonkey attriubte extension is directly about the information in the primary-key attribute name. The attribute extension, contains only information that is directly about the key attribute. The extension is information that is about the individual.

We can add one more attribute to this relation to make it less normalized. Let's say that only certain phones are authorized for long distance calls

```
name      extension    long_distance

Paul         10            yes

Susan        10            yes

George       14            no

Sabrina      14            no

Bill         18            yes

Karen        20            yes
```

Because of the logical structure of the data, an extension number is a fact about a person. The attribute `extension` represents a fact about the primary-key name. The extension is a number that is used by the individual.

There is only one candidate key in this relation, name. The structure of the data is simple. Each individual can uses a certain phone and users may share a phone.

`Long_distance` is not a fact about the user. `long_distance` is a fact about the phone. It is the phone that is authorized for long-distance, not the user. Another diagram will help make the relationship between these three items more clear

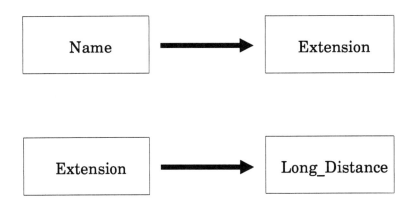

`Long_distance` is a fact about the phone. It is the phone that is authorized, or not authorized, for long distance calls.

In a normalized relation, all other attributes of the relation should contain information about the primary key. In this example, the attribute `Long_distance` is not about the primary key name. This means that the relation is not normalized. The rules of normalization say that this relation should be split into two separate relations

```
        phone
  name      extension

  Paul          10

  Susan         10

  George        14

  Sabrina       16

  Bill          18

  Karen         20


        authorization
  extension      long-distance

     10               yes

     14               no

     18               yes
```

You can see there is not as much redundant data here with two relations. With the two new relations, if the long-distance authorization for a number changes, only one record needs to be changed in the authorization relation. In the previous relation two records would have to be changed each time an authorization changes. Each of the two relationships shown in the last diagram now apply to a separate relation.

In this example, we took one complex relation and made it into two simple relations. This is what normalization is about. Normalization told us that the relation could be better organized to reduce redundant data. Normalization also told us how to change the relation to make a more simple schema.

Normalization helps you design a schema that will represent the logical structure of your data while helping to reduce redundant data. Certain steps, described below, can always be taken to normalize an unnormalized database.

For example, Chapter 3 stated that a relation can not contain repeating groups of data and still be a relation. The example in that chapter showed that an unnormalized table of data could be changed to an equivalent normalized relation by removing repeating groups of data.

Each of the normal forms constrains a database to be more organized than the last. Each normal form must be in force before the next one can be applied. There are a series of steps that can be taken to apply successive levels of normalization to an un-normalized database.

While there are a variety of normal forms, only three are described here, first normal form (1NF), second normal form (2NF) and third normal form (3NF.). For a more complete exposition of the normal forms you should see either *An Introduction to Database Systems*, by C.J. Date, published by Addison-Wesley, (1986), or "A Simple Guide to Five Normal Forms in Relational Database Theory," by W. Kent and published in the CACM **26**, No. 2 (February 1983).

NORMAL FORMS AS GUIDELINES

Note that the normal forms are a set of guidelines for constructing a schema. There is nothing in a schema, or Informix-4GL, or the relational model that enforces normalization. The rules of normalization have been developed on-top of the relational model. You can very easily build a database that is not normalized.

WHEN NOT TO NORMALIZE

Usually, you should try to design a database that is in third normal form (third normal form is described below.) There are times, though that you don't want your database in third normal form. This will be demonstrated in examples in following sections

It is not always appropriate to normalize a database. For example, look at the next relation which contains address information.

```
name            street                  city            state   zip
Paul Mahler   1800 Market St. #257   San Francisco  CA      94102
```

This relation has five attributes, name, street, city, state and zip. In any record where the city is San Francisco, the state will be California. This relation is likely to have many duplicate city names.

We could eliminate duplicate city names in the database by splitting this single relation into two relations, a city relation and a name relation:

name

```
name            street          zip
```

city

```
zip             city            state
```

In using the data in this database, though, the street, city, and state will almost always be used together. For example, if this data is used to print a mailing list, all these fields will always appear together. Printing all the information from both relations will require joining the two relations together each time the combined data is needed.

Also, zip codes do not change very often. Separating the zip, city and state into a separate relation eliminates all the duplicate city names found in the one combined relation, but since the zip code is unlikely to change, there is no advantage to eliminating the duplicate city names.

It will almost never be necessary to go into the combined relation and change the zipcode for a city. It is not likely to be necessary to go into the combined relation and change the state name in multiple records because a city has been changed to be in a new state. The duplicate city names are not likely to change. There is duplicate information, but it doesn't really change very often, so updating is less of a problem.

There is no point in reducing the redundancy of the data to improve our ability to update when we won't be updating very often anyway. In theory, breaking the one relation into two simpler relations would reduce data redundancy and improve performance. In practice, it will only introduce additional overhead.

This shows that the normal forms are only an aid to the database designer. They are suggested guidelines for logical database design. It is not always appropriate to follow the guidelines.

FIRST NORMAL FORM

Chapter 2 described the first normal form. The first normal form (1NF) states that a relation can not contain repeating groups. That is, there are no repeating groups of data allowed in a relation. Each record must have the same number of fields. That is each tuple must have the same number of attributes. For example, take the following table of data which has several repeating groups:

```
Talking Heads Speaking in Tongues,
            Little Creatures,
            Stop Making Sense
```

Unlike the other normal forms described below, a relation must at least be in first normal form to be a relation at all.

Changing a table with repeating data groups to a relation is very simple; just replace the repeating groups with tuples. For example, the table above can be made into a 1NF (first normal form) relation by making each repeating group into a separate tuple as shown here

```
Talking Heads Speaking in Tongues
Talking Heads Little Creatures
Talking Heads Stop Making Sense
```

FUNCTIONAL DEPENDENCE

The logical structure of the data in a database is shown by the functional dependence of the data. Functional dependence shows how data is logically related to other data.

Functional dependence means that the values for two attributes are linked. The value of two attributes A and B will always be the same for any particular value of A.

For example, in your organization each individual may work for a single boss. It is important to the structure of your schema that an individual be associated with a single boss. Your schema must somehow show that the boss depends on the employee.

Look at the following simple relation with two attributes, name and boss:

```
name          boss
Paul          Sam
Susan         Sam
George        Sam
Sally         Judy
Harry         Judy
Jerry         Judy
```

In this example, the value of the attribute boss can be seen to depend on the value of the attribute name. Selecting any value for name uniquely determines a value for boss. For example, if we know that the value of name is Paul then we can determine that the value of boss is Sam.

We can show this functional dependence with a simple dependency diagram.

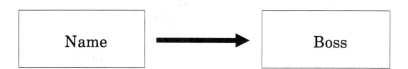

If, in your company, a person can work for two bosses, this functional dependence is lost. For example, say Paul can work for two different bosses, Sam and Judy. In this case, the relation could look like this:

```
name        boss

Paul        Sam

Susan       Sam

George      Sam

Paul        Judy

Sally       Judy

Harry       Judy

Jerry       Judy
```

This is still a relation. There is still a candidate key. The candidate key is now composed from the two attributes name and boss, {name, boss}. It is still in first normal form, there are no repeating groups. There are no duplicate tuples. It is still a relation

The boss is no longer functionally dependent on the name, though. This is because for a single value for the attribute name (Paul) there are two possible values for the attribute attribute boss (Sam and Judy.).

Please note again that the functional dependence is part of the structure of the data. Functional dependence is not part of the relational model. If Paul can only work in one department, the data in this relation is wrong. The data in the relation is wrong in the sense that it is not consistent with the logical structure of the data as it represents the real world. There is nothing in the data that makes it inconsistent with the relational model. The data still fits nicely into a relation, it just doesn't model the real world.

KEYS AND FUNCTIONAL DEPENDENCE

If an attribute is a candidate key for a relation, then all the other attributes of the relation will be functionally dependent on that attribute. This is because a candidate key uniquely selects any individual tuple.

A candidate key can uniquely select any particular tuple. The value of any other attribute will always be associated with a unique value of the candidate key. This means that all other attributes in the relation are functionally dependent on the candidate key. This means, of course, that all the other attributes of a relation are functionally dependent on the primary key of the relation.

Please note there is nothing in the definition of functional dependence that says the attribute depended on has to be a candidate key or primary key. An attribute can be functionally dependent on another attribute that is not a candidate key. For example, here is another simple relation

```
number   x   y
   1     a   1
   2     a   1
   3     a   1
```

In this relation, the attribute x is obviously not a candidate key. Still, y is functionally dependent on x. This is because we can depend on y to have the value of 1 whenever x has the value of a.

FUNCTIONAL DEPENDENCE AND COMPOSED ATTRIBUTES

An attribute can be functionally dependent on the composition of two or more other attributes. For example, look at the following relation

boss	name	department
Judy	Paul	a
Judy	Sam	a
Judy	Joe	a
Bill	Paul	b
Bill	Susan	b
Bill	Samantha	b

In this example, the department is not functionally dependent on the Name. This is because Paul is now working for two bosses in two different departments.

By putting two attributes together, that is by composing two attributes, we can achieve functional dependence. The department is functionally dependent on the composed attributes {boss, name}.

We can show this with another functional dependence diagram. The department is functionally dependent on the boss and name taken together. This is because the structure of the data specifies that any one person can only work for any one boss in a given department. That is, the department depends on the employee and the boss.

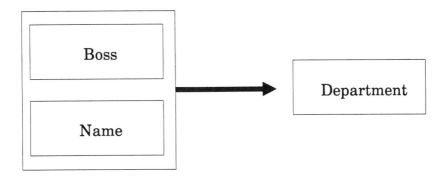

FULL FUNCTIONAL DEPENDENCE

When working with composed keys, there is another kind of dependence called full functional dependence. An attribute is fully functionally dependent on a composed attribute when it is functionally dependent on the composed attribute, but not functionally dependent on any part of the composed attribute. Here are some examples

```
boss    name    department

Judy    Paul        a

Judy    Sam         b

Judy    Joe         c

Bill    George      d

Bill    Susan       e

Bill    Samantha    f
```

In this example, the attribute department is functionally dependent on the composed attribute pair {boss, name}. In this data set, each employee only works in a single department. Since the department is also functionally dependent on the attribute name, it isn't fully functionally dependent on the composed attributes {boss, name}.

Here is another example

```
last_Name      first_Name   department

Mahler         Paul             1

Mahler         Susan            2

Mahler         Joe              3

Mahler         Kathy            4

Mahler         George           5

Jones          Paul             2
```

Here the attribute `department` is functionally dependent on the composed attribute pair {`last_name`, `first_name`}. The attribute `department` is not functionally dependent on either the attribute `last_name`, or the attribute `first_name`. Since the attribute `department` is functionally dependent on the composed pair of attributes, but not functionally dependent on either taken by themselves, it is fully functionally dependent.

Dependencies are an important part of understanding the structure of the data in a database. The fact that the department is fully functionally dependent on the last Name and first name means that each individual is in just one department. Since it is important to the structure of the data that an individual is in a single department, this structure must be represented somehow in the schema of the database. The structure of the data in a database can be specified by stating the functional dependencies.

SECOND NORMAL FORM

For a relation to be in second normal form (2NF), it must be in first normal form, and every nonkey attribute must be fully dependent on the primary key.

In the example below is a relation we used earlier which has two attributes, `name` and `extension`.

name	extension
Paul	10
Susan	10
George	14
Sabrina	16
Bill	18
Kathy	20

This relation is in first normal form; there are no repeating groups. This relation is also in second normal form because the nonkey attribute extension is a fact about the key attribute name.

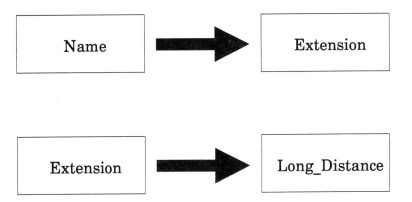

Let's add another attribute to this relation that is about the primary key, an attribute about the individual's starting time. This attribute will be called early. This attribute early will indicate if the individual starts work early, or late.

name	extension	early
Paul	10	yes
Susan	10	no
George	14	yes
Sabrina	16	yes
Bill	18	yes
Kathy	20	yes

This new attribute also is about the primary key. An individual is authorized to start work early or late. This means that adding the new attribute to the relation has not changed it from being in 2NF.

Here is the relation with the `long_distance` attribute added again:

```
name      extension    long-distance

Paul         10           yes

Susan        10           yes

George       14           no

Sabrina      14           no

Bill         18           yes

Karen        18           yes
```

This relation is no longer in 2NF. This is because the attribute `long_distance` is not about the primary key name. The attribute `long_distance` is about the extension. Here is the dependence diagram for this relation again:

We can change the 1NF relation into two 2NF relations by projecting the original 1NF relation to eliminate any non full functional dependencies. In plain English, you just break the 1NF relation into two 2NF relations where each relation has a primary key and attributes that are about that primary key. Separating the data results in two 2NF relations because each of the new relations has more simple functional dependencies. The result is as follows

phone

name	extension
Paul	10
Susan	10
George	14
Sabrina	16
Bill	18
Karen	20

authorization

extension	long-distance
10	yes
14	no
18	yes

The change from one 1NF relation into two 2NF relations can be predicted from the functional dependency diagram above. Each of the two dependencies shown in the diagram is moved to its own relation. The diagram shows that the 1NF relation has two different functional dependencies. Splitting the 1NF relation creates a new relation for each of the dependencies.

THIRD NORMAL FORM

In a 2NF relation, all the nonkey attributes must be fully functionally dependent on the primary key. A relation must be in 2NF form before it can be in 3NF form. In a 3NF relation, all the nonkey items have to be mutually independent. The nonkey attributes are all mutually independent if none of them are functionally dependent on each other. That is, for a relation to be 3NF, none of the nonkey attributes can be functionally dependent on any of the other nonkey attributes.

Here is a new relation with three attributes, `supplier`, `status`, and `city`.

supplier	city	status
s1	Detroit	10
s2	Boston	20
s3	Boston	20
s4	Dallas	30
s5	Dallas	40
s6	Detroit	10

In this set of data, each supplier is in a certain city. In addition, each city has a specified status. The status depends on the city. The city depends on the supplier and the status depends on the city. Because the city depends on the supplier and the status depends on the city, the status also depends on the supplier. The status only depends on the supplier through the city though. The dependency diagram for this relation is

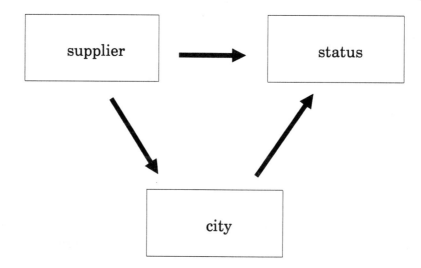

This kind of dependency makes updating the relation more difficult than it might be. In this relation with its mutual dependency, if the status changes for a city, every record for a given city must

be changed. Inserting a new record can be difficult. We can't add a record to note that a certain city has a particular status until there is a supplier for that city. For example, we can't add the information that San Francisco has status of 70 until there is a supplier for San Francisco. Deleting the only tuple for a particular city looses two items of information: the information that a supplier is in a certain city, and the information that a city has a certain status.

We can solve this problem by projecting the 2NF relation into two 3NF relations. We can separate each of the functional dependencies off into its own relation. The two resulting relations will look like this

```
    r1

supplier     city      status
   S1      Detroit       10
   S2      Boston        20
   s3      Boston        20
   s4      Dallas        30
   s5      Dallas        40
   s6      Detroit       10

    r2

city           status
Detroit          10
Boston           20
Dallas           30
```

Each of these two relations is 3NF. Each relation is 1NF because there are no repeating groups. Each relation is 2NF because all the nonkey attributes are functionally dependent on the primary key. Each is 3NF because no nonkey attribute is functionally dependent on another nonkey attribute. It is in 3NF form because each of the attributes are mutually independent.

In general, relations with simple dependencies are easier to work with. This is because they are easier to update. This is the benefit of the normal forms. The normal forms are guidelines that help you assure that relations, and a schema, are structurally simple.

SUMMARY

This chapter has introduced two important concepts. The first is functional dependency. Functional dependency demonstrates how data is logically structured. The second concept is normalization. The normal forms offer guidelines that allow you to structure a database so that the data dependencies within relations are simple.

Three normal forms were introduced, 1NF, 2NF, and 3NF. Each of these forms is more organized than the one before. Each normal form constrains a schema to have less complex data dependencies within relations. A series of steps were shown which can be used to successively reduce the complexity of a schema.

Tables that are not in 1NF form can be reduced to 1NF relations by eliminating repeating groups of data.

1NF relations with nonfull functional dependencies can be projected to produce a set of 2NF relations.

2NF relations that have inter-dependencies between nonkey attributes can be projected to produce a collection of 3NF relations.

Data dependency diagrams can be used to assist in determining the various data dependencies within a relation.

CONCLUSION

There are other normal forms. They include Boyce-Codd Normal form, 4NF, and 5NF. Each of these normal forms also presents a guideline for reducing the complexity of a database. They are beyond the scope of this introduction, however.

This chapter should leave you with the feeling that it is better to have less complex relations and thus a less complex schema. You can achieve this goal simply by remembering it is better to build a database where all the nonkey attributes in any relation only contain information that is about the primary key of the relation.

7

Informix-4GL Overview

Informix-4GL has two parts, a programming language and a programming support environment. The programming language translates high-level instructions that make sense to a programmer into low level commands that the computer can perform. The programming support environment aids the development of 4GL programs.

THE 4GL PROGRAMMING LANGUAGE

The 4GL programming language accepts a file containing a series of program statement and produces a runable program. For example, to create a database for the first time, you can write a very simple program like the following.

```
main
create database music
end main
```

Informix-4GL will translate these three statements into all the operations needed to create an empty database named `music`.

A file named `music.4gl` can hold these three commands. The Informix-4GL compiler can take this file containing commands and produce a ruinate program called `music.4ge`. Running the program `music.4ge` creates the music database. A later section shows the details of performing these steps.

THE 4GL SUPPORT ENVIRONMENT

4GL includes a programming language and a programming environment. You can write 4GL programs with the text editor of your choice and compile them with the programming language.

The 4GL environment makes it easier to write programs, compile them, run them, and fix them. You can select editing, compiling and modification commands from menus presented by the programming environment.

INFORMIX-4GL AND SQL

SQL is an acronym for Structured Query Language. SQL is an industry standard language used for manipulating and accessing a database. The 4GL environment can directly access the SQL language with a menu choice.

4GL also provides all the capabilities of SQL from within the 4GL language. 4GL language operations have a different syntax than SQL.

4GL LANGUAGE OPERATIONS

The following figure shows the operations available to the 4GL programmer. Informix-4GL provides commands for building a database, changing a database, and accessing a database. Informix-4GL provides on-screen display of windows, menus, forms, or data and provides commands for formatting and presenting data as printed reports.

4GL provides other useful functions. For example, 4GL commands access system services like the time of day or date. It also provides commands for maintaining data security and integrity. These include commands for creating and maintaining transaction logs and audit trails.

You can start by writing a 4GL program that creates a database. Then you can write another program that puts a form on screen Data can enter the database through this form. You can write another program to select data from the database and write a report.

PROGRAM ORGANIZATION

A 4GL program consists of a series of 4GL statements. Statements each have a specific format and perform a certain function. Various statement are available to perform each of the 4GL operations described above. Here is a short sample program

```
main
   define a_var integer
   let a_var =  2
   display "Hello, the variable = ", a_var
end main
```

The first line tells the 4GL compiler that a main module is starting. The second line define a_var integer, creates a variable named a_var. An_integer is a name for a place that data, an integer value in this case, can be stored. The third line stores the value 2 into the variable a_var. The fourth line displays a short message Hello, the variable = and the value held in an_integer, 2. The last line tells the 4GL compiler that the program is at an end.

STATEMENT FORMAT

4GL statements are free-form. Spaces and line breaks generally have no effect. For example, the following statements are treated identically

```
define an_integer


define
  an_integer
```

COMMENTS

Comments should always be used to explain anything that is not self-evident in a program. Comments can appear anywhere in a 4GL program. A comment starts with the pound sign # and continues to the end of the current line. Here are examples of comments

```
main # A comment can come anywhere
# after the pound sign.
# use comments wherever a program
# explanation is needed
define ax integer # A description could go here
end main
```

PROGRAM MODULES

Program statement can be grouped into modules. There must be a main program. In addition there can be functions and reports. Here is a 4GL program in outline

```
global data
main routine
one or more functions
one or more reports
```

Here is a short 4GL program that doesn't do anything. This sample program will not compile; it is only shown to demonstrate each type of program module

```
main
   call function one()
   call function two()
   output to report one()
   output to report two()
end main
#
function one()
end function one
#
function two()
end function two
#
report one()
end report
#
report two ()
end report
```

The main module, like any other module, contains 4GL statements. There must be a main module. The 4GL statements found in the main module include statements which can invoke one or more of the other modules.

A function is a series of 4GL statements written to perform some specific action and combined into a separate unit. There may optionally be one or more functions in a program. There do not have to be any functions. Functions can not include other functions.

Functions make it easier to write and correct programs. With functions, program structure can reflect program use. A function written for a common purpose is usable in many places. Program segments can be reused instead of rewritten.

Reports are a special type of function used for printing data in a specified format. Reports can not contain other reports or functions.

The main module can call functions or reports into action. Control can pass back to the main program when a report or function is complete. Functions may call other functions into action. Functions can start reports. Report routines can call functions.

Data may be passed to a function or report routine when it is called into action. Data may be returned from a function at its completion.

COMPONENTS OF A 4GL PROGRAM

This next sections describe the components of the 4GL programming language. The following chapters describe each of these language facilities at length.

DATA

Informix-4GL can combine and compare numbers, characters and Boolean (logical true and false) values.

Numbers

4GL performs math operations with numbers including addition, subtraction, multiplication and division.

Characters

A string is a group of characters, for example "abcde" or "This is a string." 4GL can combine characters into strings.

One character can be compared to another character. A string of characters can be combined with another string of characters. Part of a string of characters can be selected.

Boolean (Logical) values

Boolean values are `true` and `false`.

VARIABLES

Program variables hold data that changes over time. Variables can hold numbers or characters or Boolean values.

```
a = 1
b = "x"
c = true
```

Variables hold the results of mathematical or character or Boolean expressions.

```
a = b + c
b = "c","d"
c = true
```

SCOPE OF DATA

A variable can be defined within a module

```
main
  define var_1 integer
  call demo()
end main
function demo ()
  define var_2 integer
end demo
```

Variables can only be accessed from inside the module where they are defined. In this example, any 4GL statement in the main module could use the variable var_1. Also in this example, any statement in the function could access the data held in the variable var_2. For example, the following program assigns each of the variables a value

```
main
  define var_1 integer
  let var_1 = 2
  call demo()
end main
function demo ()
  define var_2 integer
  let var_2 = 2
end function
```

This is called scope of control. The scope of control of the variable var_2 is the function demo. The scope of control of the variable var_1 is the main module. For example, the following program will not compile or run

```
main
  define var_1 integer
  call demo()
end main
function demo ()
  define var_2 integer
  let var_2 = 2
  let var_1 = 2
end function
```

This program will not work because the function demo does not know about the variable var_1.

Any module can contain data that only it can access. Data that only a single module can access is called local data.

A global data area holds data that can be referenced by any module in a program. A program does not require a global data section. Below is an example of a program with a global data area

```
globals
define
  var_1, var_2 integer,
end globals
main
  let var_1 = 2
  call demo()
end main
function demo ()
  let var_2 = 2
end function
```

Each of the modules in this program knows about the two variable var_1 and var_2. This is because the variables are global to the two routines. Any other function or program included in this program would know about the two global variables.

PREDEFINED OPERATIONS

Predefined commands include string manipulation and access to the time of day. For example, today's date is available with the built-in operation

```
let a_var = today
```

Predefined facilities manipulate help files and react to error conditions. These are just some of a variety of useful predefined operations.

FLOW OF CONTROL

One operation is selectable from several possible operations in a 4GL program. Operations or groups of operations are repeatable any number of times. The statements that control alternation or repetition or call reports or functions determine the flow of control of a program. For example, the following instructions would do one thing if the variable a contains a Boolean value of true and something else if it contains a Boolean value of false

```
if a=true then
  do this
else
  do this instead
end if
```

SCREEN INTERACTION

A variety of 4GL statement are available for displaying or entering data to a screen. Included are commands for displaying and manipulating forms and menus.

REPORT GENERATION

4GL provides statement useful for formatting data as printed reports. A program can collect data form the user or from a database and call a report to format the data for presentation.

ERROR AND EXCEPTION HANDLING

4GL can control the flow of control of a program when an error or exception is detected. Statements provide the ability to catch errors that might cause a program to fail. An appropriate action can be taken when an error occurs rather than having a program stop completely.

8

Running Informix-4GL

There are two different Informix-4GL systems: Informix-4GL (I4GL) and the Informix-4GL rapid development system (R4GL).

The rapid development system (R4GL) provides an interactive correction facility (a debugger) in addition to the base 4GL system. Programs compile faster with the rapid development system at the expense of running slower. Programs function identically in both environments.

The standard 4GL system requires a C language compiler. The rapid development system does not need a C compiler to produce working programs. Both systems look the same to the user. The R4GL system compiled all the examples in this book. You can use either 4GL or R4GL to run each of these examples.

Each of the examples, along with other useful materials, can be ordered on disk with the form in the back of this book.

The rapid development system speeds development. When a program is completed to your satisfaction with the rapid development system, you can then re-compile it with standard 4GL to run faster.

INSTALLING INFORMIX-4GL

This chapter assumes the correct installation of Informix-4GL or the rapid development system. To insure the correct installation of Informix-4GL, consult your system administrator or the Informix supplied documentation.

You enter a computing environment when you log on to your computer or start your DOS computer. This environment includes a list of useful information held in environment variables. Some of these variables contain information that 4GL or R4GL need to operate.

For example, four environment variables must be set before Informix-4GL will operate correctly with UNIX: TERM, EDITOR, DBPATH, and INFORMIXDIR. TERM gives the type of terminal. EDITOR states which text editor you use. DBPATH lists directories to search for databases. INFORMIXDIR gives the location of Informix supplied programs.

STARTING 4GL

To start Informix-4GL, type i4gl at your system prompt. To start the rapid development system, type r4gl. After a short information display you will see a screen that looks like this:

```
INFORMIX-4GL:  Module  Form  Program  Query-language  Exit
Create, modify or run individual 4GL program modules.
─────────────────────────── Press CTRL-W for help
```

This is the main screen for 4GL or R4GL. It shows a menu with five possible choices. The R4GL menu has an additional sixth choice for calling the interactive debugger. Notice the highlighted selection Module. This shows the choice Module is selected. Move this highlight with the space bar or arrow keys. Typing a space moves the selection from one item to another. The choice Module is selected after the choice Exit. This wrapping makes the menu a ring-menu. Choices appear one at a time in a circle or ring. This means that the first choice will be selected again after you leave the last choice.

The information bar under the menu says Press CTRL-W for Help. You can try that now, if you like. Press and hold the CTRL key on your keyboard. While holding down the CTRL key, press the w key.

You now see a screen containing help information. This screen describes the choice selected on the main menu. For example, with the selection Module, help describes the choices for manipulating 4GL modules. Pressing the key marked either RETURN or ENTER on your keyboard clears the help menu.

Two different methods select menu choices on a ring menu. Pressing the ENTER key selects the highlighted menu choice. Pressing the key for the first letter of the selection name also chooses a menu item. For example, at the main menu typing m selects Module, and e selects Exit.

Exit will stop the 4GL system. Query-language starts the Informix-SQL processor. Program starts a system useful for creating and maintaining larger 4GL programs. Form provides screen-form creation and change. Module creates or changes 4GL programs. The R4GL menu has an additional choice, Debug. Debug starts the rapid development system interactive debugger.

CREATING A PROGRAM

At the main menu, type m for module. You will see a new ring menu

```
MODULE:  Modify  New  Compile  Program_Compile  Run  Exit
Change an existing 4GL program module.


———————————————————— Press CTRL-W for help ————
```

CTRL-w is always available for help. Typing e for exit returns to the previous menu. Run starts an existing 4GL program. Program_Compile builds a large program from all its subroutines and functions. Compile prepares a single program, an individual function or a group of functions or subroutines. New starts the entry of a new 4GL program. Modify provides for program changes.

Type n for new. The following screen appears:

```
NEW MODULE >
Enter the name you want to assign to the module, and press return.
───────────────────── Press CTRL-W for help ──────
```

The prompt asks for a name. Type in test and then press the enter key. This creates a module named test.4gl. The 4GL environment automatically appends the suffix .4gl to the file name. If you look in your directory later, you will see a file named test.4gl

The selected text editor will start now. On some systems, you will first see the following menu

```
USE-EDITOR >vi
Enter editor name. (RETURN only for default editor).
───────────────────── Press CTRL-W for help ──────
```

The default editor varies from one system to another. It may be vi or ed or emacs for UNIX and edlin for DOS. If you like the editor shown, type enter. You may type in a different name. For example, if you are a UNIX user, the default choice may be vi. If you prefer emacs, you can type the name for emacs on your system.

After your editor appears on-screen, type in the following short program

```
main
   create database test
end main
```

Save the file using the your editors commands. You then see the following screen

```
NEW MODULE: Compile  Save-and-exit  Discard-and-exit
Compile the 4GL module specification.
────────────────────────── Press CTRL-W for help ──────
```

Typing d discards the program and returns you to the previous menu. Typing s saves the program in a file called test.4gl and returns you to the previous menu. Typing c compiles the program you have just written.

Press c for compile. If you are using 4GL, the following menu will appear:

```
COMPILE MODULE:  Object  Runable  Exit
Create object file only; no linking to occur.
────────────────────────── Press CTRL-W for help ──────
```

Exit returns you to the previous menu. Object compiles part of a program for later inclusion into a complete program. Runable takes the program and compiles it into a running, stand-alone program. Type r for runable. The R4GL menu does not have as many choices.

If you are using 4GL, and not R4GL, you see different messages on the bottom of the screen as the compilation proceeds through three phases. The message will say compilation in progress (Phase 1) . . . please wait. With R4GL there is only one phase.

With 4GL, the first phase translates the program you have written into an ESQL program. ESQL is the proprietary Informix embedded SQL language. The second phase translates the esql program into a C program. The third phase compiles the C program to create a runable program.

With R4GL, the source program is compiled into an interpretable pseudocode (p-code.) The R4GL interpreter runs the p-code.

After compilation you see the following menu with `Run` highlighted

```
MODULE: Modify New Compile Program_Compile Run Exit
Run an existing 4GL program module or application program.

──────────────────────── Press CTRL-W for help ──────
```

Press the `enter` key. You see the following menu:

```
RUN PROGRAM >
Choose a 4GL program with Arrow Keys or enter a name, and press RETURN.
──────────────────────── Press CTRL-W for help ──────
```

Press the `enter` key to run the program you have written and compiled. The screen goes blank for a brief period as the program runs. You then see a message on the bottom of the screen `Press Return to continue`. When this message appears, press the `enter` key.

Congratulations! You have written and run your first Informix-4GL program.

The running program creates a new directory called `test.4GL.` in your current directory. This directory contains the 18 files of the empty test database.

Now, enter the following program and run it. This program erases the test database. Name it `test2`. This program displays a message on your screen when it runs.

```
main
   display "Drop test database"
   drop database test
end main
```

This completes the process of entering, compiling, and running a 4GL program. You may do this again for any of the examples in the following chapters. Create and run programs of your own with these steps too.

COMPILING PROGRAMS DIRECTLY

Programs can be compiled directly from your operating system prompt without starting the 4GL system. To compile a program directly, use the c4gl command. The Informix supplied documentation describes this command and its arguments. Direct compilation is not available with the rapid development system.

9

Defining and Using Data

This chapter describes each 4GL data type. They are numbers, dates, and characters.

A database stores each type of data. 4GL programs represent data as user-specified constant values, predefined constant values, or variables. Variables and constants are combined in expressions to create new data values. Arrays can hold multiple instances of a single data type. Records hold multiple, different data types.

NUMBERS

4GL uses five types of numbers: integer, serial, real, decimal, and money.

Integers

Integer numbers do not have a decimal portion, for example, 1, 123, 953, or –24. 4GL allows small integers and large integers. Integer values can grow larger than small integer values. Integers can be bigger than small integers because they are given more storage space. A following table shows the range of values that integer and small integers can assume.

Serial Numbers

Serial numbers provide a unique identifier for each of the records in a relation. Serial numbers are stored as the same size as integers. Serial numbers are different than integers because their values are supplied automatically by 4GL. Only one attribute in a relation can be a serial type.

Serial numbers are assigned in sequence when records are added to a relation. Each new serial number is created by adding one to the last serial number assigned.

You may select the starting serial number. If you do not select a starting serial number, the serial numbers start at one. Following serial numbers will increase by one at-a-time.

When the last serial number is reached, the serial numbers start over again at one, or whatever starting number you specified. Serial numbers cannot repeat. It is very unlikely that you will run out of serial numbers.

Real Numbers

Real number have a fractional, or decimal, part. For example, 1 is an integer and 1.1 is a real number. Math operations with real numbers are not always exact. When using very large or very small values, real arithmetic can be error prone. This is due to rounding errors that vary from machine to machine.

4GL divides real numbers into small real numbers and large real numbers. Real numbers take more storage space than small real numbers. Because of this additional storage space, real numbers can be larger than small real numbers.

Decimal Numbers and Money

Decimal numbers, and money, also have a decimal part. They are more exact than real numbers. This is because they are assigned arbitrarily large amounts of space for storage and do not have rounding errors.

Decimal numbers and money are assigned a storage length when they are created. The declaration specifies how many decimal places are to be used for the whole part of the number and how many places are to be used for the fractional part of the number. For example, decimal(8,2) specifies a decimal number with eight places to the left of the decimal point and two to the right of the decimal point. money(6,3) provides values up to $999,999.999 or as small as -$999,999.999.

Characters

Characters are held in strings. The maximum length of a character string is determined when it is declared. For example, char(10) provides space for a character string up to 10 characters long. One is the minimum size of a character string. Even a null character string must occupy at lease one character position.

Dates

Dates are entered in a variety of formats 06/01/86, or 6-1-86, or 6.1.86. Whatever format is used, dates must be entered in the order month-day-year. There is no way to change the entry order of dates to another order, like day- month- year.

Dates are displayable in different formats. The DBDATE environment variable determines the display format for a date. This is described in Appendix C of the reference manual. For example, dates are displayed in European format when the DBDATE environment variable is MDY4. European format shows as day, month, year with periods separating each.

Dates saved as integers are held internally as the number of days since December 31, 1899.

Null Values

The special value null specifies an undetermined numeric or character value. Null indicates an unknown character value that is different than a string of blanks. Null also indicates a numeric value that is not zero and unknown.

Each data type can assume a null value. The null value is stored as a special internal representation for each data type. You must specify that an attribute can accept null values when you create the attribute in the database.

DATA VALUES AND STORAGE REQUIREMENTS

The following table shows each types of numeric data and how much storage space it takes:

Type	Values	Storage Space (in bytes)
integer	-2,147,483,647 to +2,147,483,647	4
smallint	-32,767 to +32,767	2
serial	same as integer	4
float	machine dependant	8
smallfloat	machine dependant	4
decimal	arbitrarily large	see below
money	arbitrarily large	see below
char	arbitrarily large	1/character

Money or decimal storage lengths depend on their defined length. A decimal or money value takes one byte of storage for every two decimal places declared plus one additional byte for overhead.

PROGRAM DATA: CONSTANTS

A 4GL program can express numbers as a constant value, for example 1.2, 3 or 256. These individual numbers are called constants.

4GL can specify dates as constants like: "01/01/90". 4GL can express characters as a constant. For example: "ABCDE".

PROGRAM DATA: PREDEFINED CONSTANTS

4GL provides a variety of predefined constant values.

null

Null can be used in a 4GL program to provide a null character string or numeric value.

```
let A = null
```

Booleans

4GL provides two Boolean values, true and false. Null is also useable as a Boolean value. Boolean values can be combined in Boolean expressions as described in a later section on expressions. The Boolean values true and false can be stored as either integers or small integers. In this example:, the variable A must be defined as either and integer or a small integer.

```
let A = true
```

There is no separate Boolean type for variables in a 4GL program. There is no Boolean type for an attribute in a relation. Attributes and variables hold Boolean values as integers or small integers. True is stored internally as the integer 1, false is stored as the integer 0.

notfound

The predefined constant notfound is stored as an integer value of 100. For example:

```
let a = notfound
```

PROGRAM DATA: VARIABLES

4GL program variables accept and store data. The data contained in a variable can be changed over time.

```
a = 1
a = 2
```

Here the variable a takes the value 1. The variable a then takes the value 2 in the second statement.

DECLARING PROGRAM VARIABLES

A variable must be *declared* before it can be used in a 4GL program. A 4GL program variable must be assigned a type when it is declared. The define statement declares the variable and specifies the type. The following example assigns each of the possible data types to separate variables:

```
define an_integer integer
define a_small_int smallint
define a_serial
define a_float
define a_small_float smallfloat
define a_decimal decimal(6,2)
define a_money money(6,2)   # up to $999,999.99
define a_char char(10),   # up to 10 characters
define a_Boolean integer
```

These eight define statements can be shortened into one define statement. This is better programming practice. Here is the same example shown as one define statement:

```
define
   an_integer int,
   a_small_int smallint,
   a_serial ,
   a_float  float,
   a_small_float smallfloat,
   a_decimal decimal(6,2),
   a_money money(6,2),  # up to $999,999.99
   a_char char(10),  #holds up to 10 characters
   a_Boolean integer
```

NAMING PROGRAM VARIABLES

4GL program variable named can be from 1 to 18 characters in length. The first character of a variable name must be a letter. The rest of the name can include upper or lower case letters, digits, and the underscore character. Upper and lower case letters do not distinguish similar variable names. The names A_VARIABLE and a_variable identify the same variable.

4GL only uses the first eight characters of a variable name to identify the variable internally. Be careful when writing 4GL programs that the first eight characters of all different variable names are unique. In a 4GL program, the variable names a234567_x and a234567_y name the same variable.

RESERVED WORDS

There are certain names that variables cannot have. These names are reserved by 4GL for other uses. For example, a variable cannot be named smallint or real or money. An appendix presents a list of 4GL reserved words.

DATABASE DATA: DECLARING ATTRIBUTES

Each attribute found in a relation must be assigned a type. The type is assigned when the attribute is created. The following example 4GL program creates a database named test with one relation called example. This program shows the creation of an attribute for each of the nine possible data types.

```
main
create database test
create relation example (
   an_integer integer,
   a_small_int smallint,
   a_serial serial,
   a_float  float,
   a_small_float smallfloat,
   a_decimal decimal(6,2),
   a_money money(6,2),  # up to $999,999.99
   a_char char(10),
   a_boolean integer )
end main
```

Note that a_boolean is declared as an integer holds Boolean values. There is no Boolean type for an attribute in a relation. Attributes which hold Boolean values should be typed integer or small integer.

NAMING ATTRIBUTES

An attribute name can be from 1 to 18 characters in length. Attribute names must begin with a letter. The remainder of the name can include letters, digits, or the underscore character.

Case doesn't matter when naming an attribute. Each of the following programs creates an identical attribute

```
main
  create table sample (
  example char(10) )
end main

main
  create table sample (
  EXAMPLE char(10) )
end main
```

All 18 characters in a name are used to distinguish the attributes in a relation. 4GL programming is easier if the first eight characters of each attribute name are unique. This is because 4GL variable names are uniquely identified by their first eight characters.

Each of the attributes in a single relation must have a unique name. Attributes in different relations can have the same name. Do not attempt to use reserved words as attribute names. An appendix presents a list of reserved words.

EXPRESSIONS

Expressions combine constants or variables to create new data values. For example,

```
let A = B + C * 10
```

ASSIGNMENT

Data can be assigned to variables. Each of the following statements assigns a constant data value to a variable:

```
let a = 1
let a_Boolean = true
let a_Boolean = false
let a_Boolean = null
```

```
let return_status = notfound
let a_real = 4.0
```

Variables can also assume the value of other variables.

```
let a =  b
let b = a_boolean
let c =  a_real
```

NUMERIC EXPRESSIONS

Numeric variables and constants can be added, subtracted, multiplied, divided, or raised to a power. In addition, the modulus operator provides remaindering. For example, 25 mod 4 produces 1, the fractional part left over after 25 is divided by 4.

Each arithmetic operation is performed with an operator. In order of precedence, the operators are

**	exponentiation
*	multiplication
/	division
mod	modulus
+	addition
-	subtraction

Here are some examples

```
b + c
a / 2
1 + 2 + 3 + 4
123.4 / 56.2
2**2
4 mod 2
```

EVALUATION ORDER AND PRECEDENCE

Each of these operations is performed in order of *precedence*. The previous illustration shows the operators in order of precedence since exponentiation is performed in an expression before other math operations. Multiplication, division, or the modulus are performed after exponentiation but before any addition and subtraction. Operators of equal precedence are evaluated from left to right. For example, examine the following expression:

```
1 + 2 + 9 * 2/3**2
```

The constant 3 is first raised to the second power resulting in the value 9. Exponentiation has the highest precedence. Next 9 and 2 are multiplied together yielding a value of 18. This result, 18, is divided by 9 resulting in the value of 2. Then 1 and 2 are added together producing 3. Then 3 and 2 are added together to produce 5.

An expression can be evaluated in different order, or displayed with greater clarity with parentheses.

```
1 + 2 + (6 + 3) * 2/(3**2)
```

Here 3 is more clearly exponentially before the division is performed. 6 is added to 3 before the multiplication is performed.

EXPRESSION EVALUATION AND DECIMAL ARITHMETIC

All the arithmetic in an expression is carried out with decimal numbers. All the data elements of the expression are converted to decimal before they are used in computing the expression. The results of the expression are converted back to the appropriate type before being stored in the variable that hold the result. For example, if the results of an expression are stored in an integer variable, the result of the expression will be automatically converted back to type integer. Types are converted to decimal as shown here

```
This type          is converted to

float              decimal(16)

smallfloat         decimal(8)

integer            decimal(10,0)

smallint           decimal(5,0)
```

CHARACTER EXPRESSIONS

Characters can be assigned to variables with the `let` statement.

```
let a = "This is a string"
```

In addition, there are four character string operators

`,`	concatenation
`clipped`	drop trailing blanks
`[a,b]`	substring
`using`	formatting to order

Concatenate Strings

The concatenation operator combines two strings into one string.

```
let a_char_string = "abcd" , "efgh"
```

which leaves the value abcdefgh in the variable a_char_string.

Clip a String

The clipped operator strips the trailing blanks from a string. The expression

```
"123     " clipped
```

produces the string "123" which has no trailing blanks.

Select Part of a String

The substring operator selects part of a string. Note this operator will not work on a constant value. For example, take the string "123456789" held in a variable named a_string. The third and fourth characters are selected from this string with

```
a_string[3,4]
```

Here the substring operator results in the new string "34".

Format a String

The using operator changes the format of a string to produce a new string.

```
a_char_string using "format"
```

The character #, &, or * used in a format show each place a character can appear in the new string. They indicates a position where a character can be placed in the new string. Asterisks result in the new string if the format is too short to show the entire string being converted.

The # character causes leading blanks to be placed in the new string for every space not occupied by a non-space character. An ampersand (&) results in leading zeros, an asterisk (*) results in leading asterisks. For example, below the string "10000" is formatted with variety of format strings containing the # character

```
format string              resulting string
#                          " *                    "
##                         " **                   "
###                        " ***                  "
####                       " ****                 "
#####                      "10000                 "
######                     " 10000                "
#######                    "  10000               "
########                   "   10000              "
#########                  "    10000             "
##########                 "     10000            "
###########                "      10000           "
############               "       10000          "
#############              "        10000         "
##############             "         10000        "
###############            "          10000       "
################           "           10000      "
#################          "            10000     "
```

Substituting the & character for the # character in the above format strings produces these results

```
" *                    "
" **                   "
" ***                  "
"1000                  "
"01000                 "
"001000                "
"0001000               "
"00001000              "
"000001000             "
"0000001000            "
"00000001000           "
"000000001000          "
"0000000001000         "
"00000000001000        "
"000000000001000       "
```

```
"0000000000001000    "
"00000000000001000    "
"000000000000001000 "
"0000000000000001000"
```

Similarly, the * character will produce leading asterisks. This is useful for check printing

```
"*              "
"**             "
"***            "
"1000           "
"*1000          "
"**1000         "
"***1000        "
"****1000       "
"*****1000      "
"******1000     "
"*******1000    "
"********1000   "
"*********1000  "
"**********1000 "
"***********1000 "
"************1000 "
"*************1000 "
"**************1000 "
"***************1000"
```

The $ character can be used to produce a leading dollar sign that floats along with the number

format string	resulting string
$	"* "
$$	"** "
$$$	"*** "
$$$$	"**** "

```
$$$$$                           " * * * * *                         "
$$$$$$                          "$10000                             "
$$$$$$$                         " $10000                            "
$$$$$$$$                        "   $10000                          "
$$$$$$$$$                       "     $10000                        "
$$$$$$$$$$                      "       $10000                      "
$$$$$$$$$$$                     "         $10000                    "
$$$$$$$$$$$$                    "           $10000                  "
$$$$$$$$$$$$$                   "             $10000                "
$$$$$$$$$$$$$$                  "               $10000              "
$$$$$$$$$$$$$$$                 "                 $10000            "
$$$$$$$$$$$$$$$$                "                   $10000          "
$$$$$$$$$$$$$$$$$                "                     $10000        "
$$$$$$$$$$$$$$$$$$               "                       $10000      "
```

The $ character used with the # character can keep the dollar sign
at the beginning of the resulting string

```
format string              resulting string
$                          " *                        "
$#                         " * *                       "
$##                        " * * *                      "
$###                       " * * * *                     "
$####                      " * * * * *                    "
$#####                     "$10000                    "
$######                    "$ 10000                   "
$#######                   "$   10000                 "
$########                  "$     10000               "
$#########                 "$       10000             "
$##########                "$         10000           "
$###########               "$           10000         "
$############              "$             10000       "
$#############             "$               10000     "
$##############            "$                 10000   "
$###############           "$                   10000 "
$################          "$                     10000 "
```

The minus sign (-) in a format prebends a minus sign to negative numbers. For example, formatting "-10000" with "#####" results in " 10000". Formatting "-10000" with with "-#####" results in the new string "-10000".

The < character is used to left justify the resulting string.

        using "<<<<<<<<<<"

would format 10000 to

        "1000   "

A period or comma may be used in a format.

        using "$###,###.##"

will convert the character string ""10000" to "$10,000.00".

COMBINING OPERATIONS

Formatting operations can be combined to achieve powerful effects.

```
let var_a = "-        "
let var_b = 10000
let var_C =  var_a clipped, var_b using "####"
```

This example will clip the trailing blanks from the var_a. It will then concatenate this value with the formatted contents of var_b. This will result in the var_a containing the string: "-10000"

TYPE CONVERSIONS

4GL automatically converts data from one type to another as needed in expressions. In expressions using mixed data types, values are converted as necessary to perform the operations specified.

```
main
  a_char_date char(10),
  an_integer_date integer
  let a_char_date = "01/01/99"
  let an_integer_date = a_char_date
end main
```

This program defines a_char_date as a character string and an_integer_date as an integer. The variable a_char_date is then assigned the value "01/01/99", shown as a constant. When the value of the character variable a_char_date is assigned to the integer variable an_integer_date the date is converted automatically to an integer.

Automatic character conversion is particularly useful when converting numbers to strings.

```
let a_string = a_number using "$###,###.##"
```

This will convert the number found in the variable a_number to a string with the format shown.

BOOLEAN EXPRESSIONS

Strings, constants and variable numeric values can compared in expressions with the following Boolean operators. A Boolean expression always has a result of true or false

```
=                    equal
!=                   not equal
< >                  not equal
>                    greater than
>=                   greater than or equal to
<                    less than
<=                   less than or equal to
is null              contains the null value
```

Here are samples of Boolean expressions that are true

```
1 < 2
3 = 3
4 > 3
```

These expressions are false. They result in a value of `false`:

```
1 =  2
2 >= 4
3 <> 3
```

Boolean expressions can use variables and constants

```
a =  b
b <  c
c <= 3 + a
```

Parentheses can be used to clarify expression evaluation

```
a =  b + (c -d)
b >  (b - c - d + (a-4)*5)
```

For string expressions the ASCII collating order is used to determine size. In this sequence, letters follow each other in alphabetical order, lowercase letters come after uppercase letters, and digits precede lower case letters in numeric order.

```
"a" <  "b"
a =  "c"
```

One date is larger than another if it falls later in time.

```
date_1 >  date_2
date_1 <  "01/01/99"
```

A Boolean expression can determine if a variable or attribute contains a null value. In this example, the variable result will contain the value true if the variable a_var contains a value of null:

```
let result = a_var is null
```

Comparing Character Strings

Character strings are compared in Boolean expressions with the following operators

```
like         one string like another
matches      one string similar to another
is null      string contains a null value
```

Like compares one string with another. It produces the value true if the two strings compared contain the same characters in every position. In the following example result is true:

```
let string1 = "123456789"
let string2 = "123456789"
let result = string1 like string2
```

Matches compares two strings. Each string must be held in a variable. Wild cards can be used to expand the possible matches. This operator is described in the section 4-33 of the Informix supplied 4GL *User's Guide*. (For those familiar with this practice, the matches operator implements regular expressions in character comparisons.)

The null operator is true when compared to a null string. For example, here result has a value of true

```
let string = null
let result = string is null
```

The sense of these operators is reversed by using not. Here are some examples which all produce a result of true:

```
let string = "abcde"
let result = string is not null
let result = string not like "123456"
```

COMPOUND EXPRESSIONS

Boolean operators can be combined into compound statements with the operators and, or, and not. The operator and produces a true value only when both expressions are true. The following examples are all true:

```
true and true
(1=1) and (2=2)
(1<2) and (2<3)
```

The or operator produces a value of true when either expression is true. The following examples are all true:

```
(1=1) or (2=2)
(1<2) or (2<2)
```

The not operator reverses the result of an expression. Not turns true to false and false to true. The following are all true:

```
not (1 = 2)
not (2 < 1)
not ((1=2) and (2=3))
```

ARRAYS

Groups of items of the same type can be held in an array. An array holds multiple elements of the same type. Each element has its own address. For example, here is an array of character strings. This array can hold five different character strings. Each character string can hold up to three characters

```
define an_array [5] of char(3)
```

An array is like a series of buckets. Each bucket has its own label or address. Each bucket can hold one data value. You can get an individual item by knowing the address of its bucket. The number of the bucket tells you where the item is stored. For this example there are five buckets numbered one to five Each of the buckets can hold a different character string. Each character string can hold up to three characters.

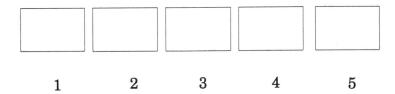

Each of the buckets, or locations, is called an *element* of the array. The address of a particular element in the array is an *index*. You can access any individual element with the name of the array and the index of the element. For example, the following shows how the string "AAA" is stored in the first element of the array

```
let an_array[1] = "AAA"
```

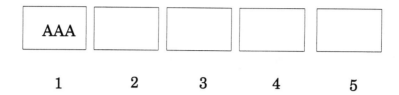

Similarly, you could put the string "BBB" in the second location like this

```
let an_array[2] =  "BBB"
```

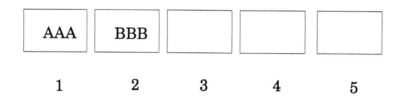

You can copy the contents of one array element to another array element. This statement will leave the string "BBB" in the third element of the array

```
let an_array[3] = an_array[2]
```

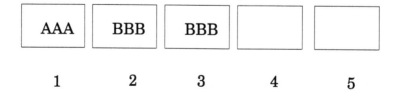

Arrays can have more than one dimension.

```
define another_array array[5,3] of integer
```

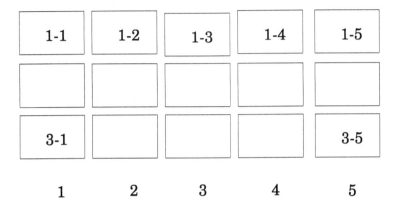

Here, two indexes are needed to identify an individual element of the array. You can think of this two dimensional array as three rows of boxes with five boxes in each row. The first index identifies the row. The second index identifies the element in that row.

Arrays can have up to three dimensions.

```
define b_array array[5,5,5] of integer
```

This array contains 125 (5x5x5) elements.

Selecting Substrings in Character Arrays

You can select a substring from one element of an array of character strings.

```
define
    an_array array[5] of char(7),
    sub_string char(5)
let an_array[1]="123bc67"
```

```
let sub_string = an_array[1] [4,5]
```

This example will leave the string "bc" in the variable
sub_string

RECORDS

A record combines a group of individual data elements into a single
named unit. The record is assigned a name when it is defined. A
record is a group of different data elements known by a single
name.

```
define
  tst_record record
    last_name char(20),
    middle_initial char(20),
    first_name char(20)
    salary money(10,3)
  end record
```

This statement creates a new record named tst_record. It has
four elements last_name, middle_name, first_name and
salary.

The record name and element name separated with a period can
address an individual value. For example, you can change the
value of the salary with this statement

```
let tst_record.salary = 1000.00
```

RECORDS LIKE RELATIONS

A record can be quickly built that is just like part or all of a relation
in a database. For example, take a relation in a database named
t_relation with the following elements

```
last_name char(20)
```

```
middle_initial char(20)
first_name char(20)
salary char(20)
```

The following statement creates a record named t_record which contains two data elements last_name and first name:

```
define
  t_record record
    lname like t_relation.last_name,
    fname like t_relation.first_name
  end record
```

Each of these data elements will have the same size and type as the data elements found in the relation. In this example, lname and fname will both be char(20).

The following statement creates a record which has as many elements as the relation t_relation:

```
define t_record like t_relation.*
```

This statement creates a new record name t_record. The new record has as many elements as the relation tst_relation. This statement above has the same effect as the following statement

```
define
 t_record record
   last_name like t_relation.last_name,
   middle_intital like t_relation_middle_intital,
   first_name like t_relation.first_name,
    salary like t+relation salary,
   end record
```

ARRAYS OF RECORDS

A statement like this one creates an array of records

```
define
  tst_array array[5] of record
    last_name char(20),
    middle_initial char(20),
    first_name char(20),
  end record
```

This statement creates an array named `tst_array` with five elements. Each of the five elements is a record with three elements `last_name`, `middle_initial`, and `first_name`.

Each of the five records is addressable. Here, the fifth record is addressed

```
let tst_array[5].last_name = "Mahler"
```

The particular record desired is selected by number, in this case five. The standard notation, a period followed by the record element id, selects the desired record element from the fifth record.

RECORDS CONTAINING RECORDS

Records can contain records.

```
main
  define
    arec record
      a char(10),
      b char(4),
      c record
        x integer,
        y integer
      end record,
      d integer
    end record
  let arec.a = "test"
  let arec.c.x = 10
end main
```

In this example, the record `arec` contains a subrecord named `c`. You can access items in the main record or subrecord as shown below.

The name of the record and the name of the element can select any individual element within the record. For example `arec.b` selects the element b within the main record `arec`. Similar notation can select elements from the subrecord c. For example, `arec.c.x` selects the element x within the subrecord c.

Records can only be created within records as shown above. You can not reference a previous record as part of a new record definition. For example, this will not work

```
define
   arec record
      a char(1),
      b integer,
      c char(10)
   end record,
   brec record
      a like arec.*
```

INITIALIZING VARIABLES AND RECORDS TO NULL

Variables and records should always be initialized before they are used for the first time. Variables can be initialized to any appropriate value with an assignment statement.

```
let a = 10
```

Variables can be intialized to `null` with the `intialize` statement.

```
define a integer
initialize a to null
```

The `initialize` statement can be used repeatedly to initialize a variable.

In this example, the intialize statement is used to repeatedly re-intialize the variable a to null before the variable is reused

```
define a integer
initialize a to null
let a = 1
initialize a to null
let a = 2
initialize a to null
let a = 3
```

The `initalize` statement can also intialize all the elements of a record to `null`.

```
main
  define xrec record
    xint integer,
    xc char(10)
  end record
  initialize xrec.* to NULL
end main
```

10

Creating and Changing a Database

This chapter describes the creation, removal, change, and indexing of a database. The chapter describes how data is entered into and taken out of a database.

CREATING A DATABASE

The `create database` statement builds a new empty database. The format of the statement is

```
create database name
```

where name is any legal name as described in the next section.

Here is a sample

```
main
   create database test1
   create database test2
   create database test3
end main
```

Please note the name of the database to be created is not enclosed in quotation marks.

The create database statement has an additional form. A character variable can name the database created. The format of this statement is

```
create database variable
```

Here is an example

```
main
  define db_name char(10)
  let db_name = "test"
  create database db_name
end main
```

The create database statement will fail if a database with the specified name already exists in the current working directory. There is no conflict if a similarly named database exists in a different directory than the current directory.

The create database statement will fail if a directory named with the database name and .dbs suffix already exists in the current working directory. The creation will fail even if this directory is empty. The create database statement must be able to create the directory containing the database.

NAMING A DATABASE

For UNIX systems, names are from one to ten characters in length. On DOS systems, names are up to eight characters long and have an additional extension of up to three characters, for example X2345678.123.

The name must start with a letter. The remaining characters can be letters, numbers, or digits. Upper and lower case letters make no difference when assigning a database name. These two statements will each make a database named test

```
create database test
create database TEST
```

Similarly, each of these statements removes a database named test

```
drop database test
drop database TEST
```

Do not attempt to use a reserved word for a database name. A list of reserved words is given as an appendix.

WHAT FILES ARE IN A DATABASE?

When a database is created, a directory is created in the current working directory. This directory name is the same as the database name with a suffix of .dbs appended. For example, a database test will be held in a directory named test.dbs.

When a database is created, a set of files is created in the database directory. These files contain user supplied data, indexes, and structural information. For example, this program creates a small test database

```
main
  create database test
  create table example (
    an_integer integer,
    a_smallint smallint,
    a_float float,
    a_small_float smallfloat,
    a_decimal decimal,
    a_money money,
    a_char char(10),
    a_boolean integer )
end main
```

This program creates a database named test. When this program is run it creates a directory named test.dbs in the current directory. The files that make up the database are then created in this directory. If a directory named test.dbs already exists, the program cannot create a database and fails.

After the program is run, the directory test.dbs holds 20 files. One file named example100.dat (on UNIX systems) will contain data added to the relation named example. This file is empty because no user data is in the database. A file named example100.idx contains indexing information for the relation example.

The 18 remaining files contain structural information about the test database. These files contain a list of all relation names and attribute names. These files also contain access authorizations and indexing information. (Appendix B of the *Informix-4GL Reference Manual* shows each system table and describes its format and function.)

OPENING A DATABASE

The database statement opens a database for use.

```
main
   database test
end main
```

4GL will search in the current working directory for a database named test. If no database named test can be found in the current directory, 4GL will search in each of the directories listed in the DBPATH environment variable. It will use the first database it finds that has the correct name. Any changes this program makes to data would be to the database named test.

The database in used by a running program is changed with the database statement. A variable may be used in this application of the database statement

```
main
  define db_name char(10)
  let db_name = "test1"
  database db_name
  let db_name = "other"
  database db_name
end main
```

This program first selects a database named test1 for data access; then it accesses a database named other. The database statements used to determine the run-time database must appear after any define statements.

AUTOMATIC DATA TYPING

4GL uses the database statement to determine which database to use for automatic typing of variables at compile time. With this usage the database statement must appear as the first statement in the program before the main module

```
database test
main
  define an_integer like table1.attr
end main
```

Here the statement database test selects the test database. The database test determines the type of the variable an_integer. 4GL looks in the database test for a relation named table1 for an attribute named attr. The variable an_integer will be given the same data type as the attribute attr found in the test database.

The test database remains selected by this statement for access by the running program. Any data access will be to the test database until the database is changed with another database statement or closed with a close database statement.

CLOSING A DATABASE

The close database statement closes the currently selected database.

```
main
   create database test
   close database
end main
```

After the close database statement, no database will be available for use.

DROPPING A DATABASE

The drop database statement removes a database entirely. This statement removes all database files and the directory containing the database files. The statement has the following format

```
drop database db_name
```

This program removes a database named test

```
main
   drop database test
end main
```

A character variable can also specify the database in a drop database statement.

```
main
   define db_name char(10)
   let db_name = "test"
   drop database db_name
end main
```

A database that is in use cannot be dropped. For example, the following program will not run correctly

```
main
  create database test
  drop database test
end main
```

The create database statement also leaves the database selected. The database cannot be dropped until it is closed. This program will run correctly

```
main
  create database test
  close database
  drop database test
end main
```

Operating system commands can also remove all the files of a database and the containing database directory. This has the same effect as the drop database statement.

CREATING RELATIONS

A relation is created with the statement

```
create table name
```

where name is any legal name as described in the next section. This statement creates a temporary relation

```
create temp table name
```

Temporary relations are automatically removed when the program that creates them stops.

NAMING RELATIONS

Relation names may be up to 18 characters long. A relation name must start with a letter. Other characters of the name can be letters, digits, or the underscore character. Upper and lower case letters do not distinguish relation names. The names CARS and cars identify the same relation.

DROPPING RELATIONS

The drop table statement removes a table or temporary table from a database. The format of the statement is

```
drop table tablename
```

where tablename is the name of any table in a database.

RENAMING A RELATION

The rename table statement changes the name of a relation

```
rename table oldname to newname
```

Here is an example

```
rename table table1 to first_table
```

CREATING ATTRIBUTES IN A NEW RELATION

The create table statement creates a new relation

```
create table table_name (
attribute_name_1 type,
attribute_name_2 type,
. . .)
```

Legal attribute name and the various data types are described in the preceding chapter. This sample program creates an attribute for every possible datatype

```
main
  create database test1
  create table table1 (
    a_char char(10),
    an_integer integer,
    a_small_int smallint,
    a_float float,
    a_decimal decimal(10,2)
    a_serial serial,
    a_money money(6,2),
    a_date date,
    a_boolean smallint )
end main
```

ADDING ATTRIBUTES TO AN EXISTING RELATION

The alter table statement adds attributes to an existing relation

```
alter table tablename add (
    name type,
    name type,
    . . .)
```

Here is an example

```
main
  create database test
  create table table1 (an_integer integer)
  alter table table1 add (a_money money(10,3) )
end main
```

The before option of the create table statement specifies the position where new attributes are placed in a table.

```
main
  create database test
  create table table1 (an_integer integer)
  alter table table1 add (a_money money(10,3) )
  alter table table 1 add (
  a_boolean smallint before a_money)
end main
```

After this example, the relation table1 will contain three attributes in the following order: an_integer, a_boolean, a_money.

DROPPING ATTRIBUTES

The alter table statement deletes attributes from a relation. The following assume a relation named table1 with three attributes

```
        an_integer integer,
        a_char char(10),
        a_boolean smallint
```

The drop statement has the format

```
        alter table tablename drop
           (attribute, attribute, . . .)
```

This drop statement removes two attributes from the relation table1

```
alter table table1 drop (an_integer, a_boolean)
```

RENAMING AN ATTRIBUTE

The rename column statement renames attributes. In a relation named test2 containing an attribute named a_char, the following statement will rename the attribute

```
rename column test2.a_char to b_char
```

Note that the attribute to be renamed must be fully qualified with the relation name. relation.attribute. Note also that the rename column statement can only rename one attribute at a time.

CHANGING THE TYPE OF AN ATTRIBUTE

The alter table statement can change an attribute from one type to another. The format of the statement is

```
alter table tablename
   modify (attribute new_type, . . .)
```

Here are two examples

```
alter table test2 modify (a_char integer)
alter table test2 modify (
   a_char char(10),
   an_integer float not null )
```

Note that if an attribute holds data, this data may be lost during some kinds of type conversions.

CREATE AN INDEX

This sections shows how to add an index to a relation. Chapter 5 tells when it is appropriate to use an index.

The `create index` statement adds an index to a relation. Only one index can be created at-a-time with the `create index` statement.

Index names have the same format as attribute names. They can be up to 18 characters in length, must start with a letter, and can contain letters, numbers, and the underscore character.The format of this statement is

```
create index index_name on table_name
  (column_name . . .)
```

Here is an examples

```
create index i_customer on customer
  (customer_name)
```

The following statement creates an index named i_customer. It is an index on the customer_name field of the customer table. This index would speed access to the database when looking for customers by their last name.

This index would speed access to data held in increasing alphabetical order. As the relation contains more data this index will speed access to data when searching on the customer name.

Indexes created in this manner are kept in ascending numeric or alphabetical order. With this index it is fastest to find customers with names that are in earlier alphabetical order. Data to be shown in a report in increasing alphabetical order can be found more quickly when indexed in ascending order.

DESCENDING ORDER

Where data is to be searched from larger to smaller rather than smaller to larger, a descending index should be used.

```
create index i_order_number
    on orders (order_number desc)
```

This index would speed access to data where smaller order numbers are accessed more frequently than larger order numbers. This index would also speed reporting where reported data is shown in descending order by order number.

COMPOSITE INDEX

A composite index is an index created for multiple columns in a relation. This statement creates a composite index

```
create index i_nc on customer (fname, city)
```

The two attributes fname and city are used together to create an index. This index will speed access to the relation for searches based on a combination of fname and city.

A composite index can be created with a combination of ascending and descending orders.

```
create index i_nc on customer
    (fname, fnum desc)
```

Here access is speeded to fname in ascending order and fnum in descending order.

UNIQUE INDEX

A unique, or distinct, index can be created for an attribute. In this case, no duplicate values will be allowed for that attribute. This prevents the addition of duplicate data values to a relation. When an attribute has a unique index, any attempt to add a duplicate data value to the database for this attribute will fail. Here is an example where a unique index is added to a relation

```
create unique index i_customer_num
    on customer (customer-num)
```

The keyword distinct can be used in place of the keyword unique.

```
create distinct index i_customer_num
    on customer (customer-num)
```

DROPPING AN INDEX

The drop index statement will remove indexes from a relation. Only one index can be removed with a single drop index statement. Here are some examples.

```
drop index i_customer_num
drop index i_fname
drop index city
drop index state
```

11

Accessing the Data in a Database

This chapter demonstrates how data is manipulation in a database. The first section shows how an individual record can be selected with the select statement. Later sections show how a group of records can be selected and manipulated with the select statement and a cursor. This chapter also shows how tables in a database can be locked and unlocked to prevent simultaneous access. Finally, database permissions are described.

THE SELECT STATEMENT

The select statement retrieves one or more rows of data from a relation. This process of selecting data from a database is often called a query.

The next section describes how to use the select statement to retrieve a single row of data from a database and leave the data found in program variables. Later sections describe how to select multiple rows of data with a select statement and access them with a cursor.

SELECTING SINGLE RECORDS FROM A DATABASE

The select statement is divided into several clauses. Each clause describes part of the operation of the select statement. A select-list describes which attributes to retrieve from a database. A variable-list describes which program variables will receive the data retrieved from the database. A table-list shows which tables will be joined and searched for the attributes. Finally, various search-conditions give the criteria used for selecting the appropriate rows of data from the named tables. Here is the format of a select statement used to select a single row from a relation:

```
select select-list into variable-list
  from table-list where search-conditions
```

Below is an example of a select statement that selects one row from the stores database. The stores database is the example database in the Informix supplied documentation. Running the command i4gldemo from your operating system prompt will create a demonstration database for you in your current working directory.

```
database stores
main
  define c_num like customer.customer_num
  select customer_num into c_num from customer where
customer_num = 101
  display "Customer Number =", c_num
end main
```

This program opens the stores database. It then looks for a row in the customer relation where the customer number is equal to 101. When it finds this row, if one exists, it retrieves the value for the customer_num attribute and leaves it in the program variable named c_num. The display statement shows on-screen the value left in the program variable c_num.

There is nothing in this select statement that restricts it to finding a single row in the database. This statement will find all the records in the relation that have a customer number of 101.

The select statement must return only one value for the program containing it to work correctly. This is because there is only one variable for data to be retrieved into, c_num. For example, this program will fail because the select statement will find more than one row of data in the database where the state is California:

```
database stores
main
   define c_number like customer.customer_number
   select customer_number into c_number
     from customer where state = "CA"
end main
```

Any select statement with an into clause that is used in a 4GL program is expected to find only one row of data. If more than one row is found, the program containing the select statement will fail. If you try to run the sample program above, you will see an error message that says: a subquery has returned not exactly one value.

WERE ROWS FOUND?

Note that if a query fails, the variables in the into clause are left unchanged. Also, if the select statement does not find any rows, the built-in program variable status will be set to the built-in value notfound. The following program will display a message if no rows are found.

The if statement in this program will display a message if the value left in the variable status is equal to the value of the built-in constant notfound. (As a built-in constant, the value of notfound is always 100.) The if statement is discussed at greater length in the following chapter on flow of control.

```
database stores
main
  define c_num like customer.customer_num
  select unique customer_num into c_num from cus-
tomer
    where state = "MI"
  if status = notfound then
    display "No Rows Were Found"
  end if
end main
```

THE SELECT LIST

The format of the select statement is

```
select select-list
```

The select list specifies the data to be retrieved from the database. It gives a list of attributes to retrieve. A list of attributes can be given

```
select a1, a2, a3, a4
  from table_name
```

All the attributes of a relation can be selected with the * symbol

```
select * from customer
```

DISTINCT OR UNIQUE

The list of attributes to be selected from a relation in the database can be qualified with the either the modifier distinct or the modifier unique. These are synonyms and have the same effect. The distinct or unique keyword can be used to insure that duplicate rows will be eliminated from the results of a select.

```
select unique customer_num
   into c_num
   from customer
       . . .
```

If there are duplicate rows of data in the relation, this statement will insure that only one copy will be returned by the select statement.

Note that if the query finds multiple different rows, the program will still fail. The example above will fail because there is more than one record in the relation where the state is California (CA) but where other attributes are different.

THE INTO LIST

The into clause of a select specifies the program variables where retrieved data is stored

```
select * into a1,a2
```

It is the into clause that allows 4GL to determine that a single record is expected back from the database as a result of the select statement. Any select statement with an into clause is expected to return only one row. See the section following on selecting multiple records for a description of selecting multiple rows.

THE FROM LIST

The `from list` specifies the tables to be searched. A single table can be searched as follows

```
select * into a1,a2 from r1
```

The relation `r1` has two attributes. The data from these two attributes is selected into the variables `a1` and `a2`. The first attribute selected from the relation with the * will be left in the first variable `a1`. The second attribute is left in `a2`, the third in `a3`, and so on.

Two relations can be joined with the `from elist`. This will be described in a later section.

THE WHERE CONDITION

The selection of data from the database can be qualified with a `where` clause. This clause allows conditions to be applied to the selection of data from the database. , a selection can be restricted to a certain numeric range

```
select *
   into a1, a2, a3
   from test where attr1 > 100
```

This statement will select all the records in the table `test` where the value of attribute `attr1` is found to contain a value greater than `100`.

The `where` clause can be used to narrow the search for data in the database. The `where` clause can narrow the search so that only one record will be returned by a query.

Any legal Boolean expression may be used to restrict a selection. Boolean statement are described in chapter nine. Here are some examples of legal where clauses

```
where attribute > 100
where attribute > 100 and attribute < 500
where a1 = 2 and a2 = 14
where attribute is not null
where attribute is null
where attribute is between 1 and 200
```

THE UNION OPERATOR

One or more queries can be combined with the union operator.

```
select distinct stock_num, menu_code
  from stock
  where unit_price < 100.00
union
select stock_num, menu_code
  from items
  where quantity > 3
```

A union combines one or more queries into a single query. The example above can be replaced with a single query like this

```
select distinct stock_num, menu_code
  from stock
  where unit_price < 100.00 and quantity > 3
```

SELECTING MULTIPLE RECORDS

The examples in the previous sections all showed queries which returned a single row of data. A select statement can identify multiple records in a database.

```
select * from customer where customer_num >100
```

This query could return more than one record from the database. If there are two records in the `customer` table with a customer_num greater than `100`, both records will be identified by this query.

In some cases, a selection will return more than one tuple. There must be a way of to select each of the tuples that are returned by on-at a time. This mechanism is the cursor.

CURSORS

A query designed to identify multiple records in a database should not have an `into` clause. When a query is expected to return multiple records, a cursor should be used instead. The cursor can be used to point at one record at a time. With the cursor each of the multiple records returned by a query can be manipulated individually one at a time.

A `select` statement can identify a group of records in a database. The set of tuples returned by the query are called the active set. The `cursor` statement provides a mechanism for accessing each of the records in the active set one at a time, from first to last.

Here is an example of a `select` statement that can find a group of records in a database. When imbedded in a correct program with other supporting statements, this query will select all the tuples in the `state` relation

```
select * from state
```

The example query will select all the state names to be found in the `state` table in the `stores` database. The query will find 50 tuples in the `state` table, one for each state in the United States.

Even though the select statement is correct, this program will fail to run correctly

```
database stores
main
   select * from state
end main
```

This program will compile and run. It will stop and issue the message A subquery has returned not exactly one value. This is because the select statement has found more than one record satisfying the selection criteria.

This problem is fixed by using a cursor. A cursor is declared to operate with a particular select statement. A select statement is attached to cursor.

A select statement can identify a group of records within a database. The cursor can then be used to point to each of the selected records one at a time from first to last. Here is an example that attaches the select statement shown above to a cursor

```
declare c_state cursor for
   select * from state
```

This statement creates a cursor named c_state. The cursor can choose each of the records returned by the select statement select * from state. This is shown in the later section on moving a cursor.

Note that the cursor is named starting with a c_. This will make it easier to recognize it as a cursor when it is referenced in other places in the program.

OPENING AND CLOSING A CURSOR

When the cursor is opened, the select statement is automatically used to select the specified records from the database.

```
database stores
main
  declare c_state cursor for select * from state
  open c_state
  close c_state
end main
```

This program creates a cursor named c_state. This cursor is attached to the select statement select * from state.

When the cursor is opened with the open statement, the query is executed. The state table is searched to select every tuple that matches the criteria of the query. In this case, the select statement will identify 50 tuples in the state relation.

When a cursor is no longer of use, it may be closed with the close statement as shown above. Any cursor which will no longer be used should be closed. This will reduce the overhead of a running 4GL program. There is an installation-dependent upper limit to the number of cursors that can be open at any one time.

Please note that closing a cursor changes the value of the status variable. The status variable can't be relied on to have an accurate value after a cursor is closed. There is no telling what value will be left in the status variable after the cursor has been closed.

MOVING A CURSOR

After a group of records has been selected, the cursor can be moved to point to each one of them in order from first to last.

```
database stores
main
  define r_state record like state.*
  declare c_state cursor for select * from state
  open c_state
  fetch c_state into r_state.*
  display r_state.*
```

```
   close c_state
end main
```

In this example, a record called r_state is defined. This record contains all the attributes found in the state relation. Then a cursor named c_state is declared. The select statement attached to this cursor will find all the records in the state relation.

When the cursor is opened, the select statement will select all the tuples found in the state relation. The fetch statement will then fetch the first tuple found in the active set and leave the data in the r_state record.

Note that there is a record, or a set of variables, that the data is moved into. When the cursor is moved to each new record, the data found is left in a set of program variables. This program will perform the same function

```
database stores
main
   define c_rec record
     code char(2),
     sname char(15)
   end record
   declare c_state cursor for
     select * from state
   open c_state
   fetch c_state into c_rec.code, c_rec.sname
   display "Code =",crec.code," Name =",c_rec.sname
   close c_state
end main
```

Fetch statements can now move the cursor to each record found by the select statement In this example, information found in the second record returned by the query will be displayed

```
database stores
main
  define r_state record
    code char(2),
    sname char(15)
  end record
  declare c_state cursor for
    select * from state
  open c_state
  fetch c_state into r_state.code, r_state.snam
  fetch c_state into r_state.code, r_state.sname
  display "Code =",r_state.code,
    " Name =",r_state.sname
  close c_state
end main
```

DETECTING THE LAST TUPLE

The built-in status variable may be used to detect when the last tuple has been reached.

```
database stores
main
define
  c_rec record
    code char(2),
    sname char(15)
  end record
  declare c_state cursor for
    select * from state
  open c_state
  fetch c_state into c_rec.code, c_rec.sname
  fetch c_state into c_rec.code, c_rec.sname
  if status = notfound then
    display "No more records."
  else
    display "Second record found"
```

```
      end if
      close c_state
end main
```

If the second `fetch` statement fails, the value of `status` will be set to `notfound` and the message `No more records` will be displayed. If a second record is found, the message `Second record found` is displayed.

THE ORDER BY CLAUSE

Remember from relational theory that the tuples in a relation are not stored in any particular order. In my copy of the `stores` database the tuple for Alaska is first and the tuple for Hawaii is second. They could be stored in any order, however.

The records returned by a query can be ordered with the `order by` clause.

```
database stores
main
  define c_rec record
    code char(2),
    sname char(15)
  end record
  declare c_state cursor for
    select * from state order by code
  open c_state
  fetch c_state into c_rec.code, c_rec.sname
  display "Code =",crec.code," Name =",c_rec.sname
    close c_state
end main
```

This program displays the tuple for the state of Alabama because the records are ordered by state name by the `select` statement. Alabama is the second state by alphabetical order.

Records can also be returned by the `select` statement in descending order with the `desc` keyword. This statement returns the states in reverse alphabetical order

```
select * from state
  order by code desc
```

More than one attribute can be used in an order by clause

```
select * from relation
  order by attr1, attr2, attr3
```

The query will order the records found first by the first attribute named and then by each succeeding attribute. If the first attribute were a date and the second attribute a quantity the records would come first in order of date. Within each date the records would be ordered by increasing quantity.

Records can also be put in descending order when ordered by multiple attributes. This example will sort the returned records in increasing order of the first and third attributes, but by decreasing order of the second attribute

```
select * from relation
  order by attr1, attr2 desc, attr3
```

THE GROUP BY CLAUSE

The group by clause can be used in a query to reduce duplicate rows of data to a single row.

```
select order_num from items group by order_num
```

More than one attribute can be named in the group by clause.

```
group by attr1, attr2, attr3
```

The group by clause causes just a single row to be returned for each group. A group is a set of rows having the same values for each of the attributes listed in the group by clause.

THE HAVING CLAUSE

The having clause can be used with the group by clause. The having clause is similar to the where clause discussed earlier. The having clause restricts the selection to only those groups that meet the specified qualification.

```
select order_num
    from items
    group by order_num
    having order_num > 3000
```

This query will return only those groups where the order_num is greater than 3000.

SCROLL CURSORS

A simple cursor as described above can only be moved from the first record selected to the last record selected. A scrolling cursor can be moved backwards as well as forwards.You can move to the next tuple, the previous tuple, the first tuple, the last tuple, or any selected tuple of your choice.

When opened, this nonscrolling cursor will automatically select the first record returned by the query

```
 declare c_state cursor for
    select * from state order by code
```

Each time a a fetch statement is executed, the next available record will be returned. The first record found by the query will be returned by the first fetch statement. Each successive fetch will return the next record selected by the query until the last record is reached. With this cursor there is no way to move backwards through the records. The only path through the records is from the first record to the last record in the order they were selected.

This example declares a scrolling cursor

```
declare c_state scroll cursor for
    select * from state order by code
```

The scroll cursor can select the first or last record found by the select. The scroll cursor can also select the next record, or the previous record. The cursor can also select any individual record by number counting the first record found as number one. The cursor can also be moved forward or backward relative to the current record.

```
fetch first
fetch last
```

These will fetch the first record or the last record found by the select statement.

```
fetch next
fetch previous
```

Use these to move the cursor one record backwards or forwards from where the cursor is currently pointing.

```
fetch current
```

This leaves the cursor at the currently selected record

```
fetch relative n
```

This will move the cursor n records forward or backwards, for example one forward or two backward

```
fetch relative 1
fetch relative -2
```

To move to a specific record by number where the selected records are numbered from one use

```
fetch absolute n
```

for example

```
fetch absolute 100
```

The scroll cursor should only be used when the cursor will be moved at random. The scroll cursor has greater overhead than a non-scrolling cursor. If the program will always access selected records from first to last, without backing up or moving around, use the non-scrolling form of the cursor declaration.

A cursor is declared at a specific line in a source file. Any statements that are physically after the declaration can reference the cursor. This is true even if the reference is in another, later, different function.

THE FOREACH STATEMENT

You can open a cursor, and move it through each of the available records, with the `foreach` statement.

The `foreach` statement automatically opens a cursor and then moves it through all the selected tuples from first to last. The following statement would retrieve each tuple selected, one at a time. As the information contained in each tuple is retrieved, it is left in the record called `p_record`

```
foreach c_item_list into p_record.*
    (other executable statement go between
     the foreach and end foreach statements.)
end foreach
```

The foreach statement will open and close the cursor for you. It will automatically stop when the last tuple found by the query is reached.

In this example, the cursor c_item_list is opened, moved through each tuple, and then closed by the foreach statement. This example is not very useful as it leaves each tuple retrieved in the same record, one after the other. This writes each new tuple retrieved into p_record over the previous tuple

Informix provides various sample programs. They are usually found in the directory /usr/informix/demo/fgl on UNIX systems or /informix/demo/fgl on DOS systems. They may be located in other directories on your system. While these sample programs are stylistically weak, they can serve as an excellent source of examples of what can be done with Informix-4GL.

This example is drawn from the Informix supplied demo program d4_orders.4gl. There is a minor change to the Informix supplied program which will be described below.

In this example, there is an integer variable called idx. This index is used to point to successive locations in an array of records. By increasing the index by one when each tuple is retrieved, each tuple is left in a new array element of the array p_items. Note that the index must be incremented by 1 each time a tuple is retrieved with the statement let idx = idx + 1.

```
let idx = 1
foreach item_list into p_items[idx].*
  let idx = idx + 1
  if icx > 10 then
    error "More than 10 items"
    exit foreach
  end if
end foreach
let idx = idx -1
```

The index must be initialized to one before the `foreach` statement. This is so that the first tuple retrieved by the cursor will be left in array element one. If the index were initialized to zero, the `foreach` statement would attempt to place the first tuple retrieved into array location zero and fail.

This particular example is designed to retrieve only the first 10 tuples selectable by the cursor. After the tenth item, there is an exit from the `foreach` statement. The exit is programmed with the `exit foreach` statement. The `exit foreach` statement causes the `foreach` statement to stop. Control is passed to the next statement following the `end foreach` statement.

This example differs slightly from the example given in the Informix supplied demo program. The difference is that the index is decreased by one after the `foreach` statement with the statement `let idx = idx -1`.

Upon exiting the `foreach` statement, the index will be pointing to the next available array element, not the last item found. This is why the index must be decreased by one. Decreasing the index by one makes the value of the index equal to the number of rows retrieved. Note that if no records are retrieved by the `foreach` statement, the index will have a value of zero after the `let idx = idx -1` statement.

There is also no need to test for the last record when using the `foreach` statement. The `foreach` will stop automatically when the last tuple is reached.

JOINING TABLES WITH THE SELECT STATEMENT

The `music` database will be used to demonstrate joins. Here is the `music` database again

Music Database

cd

performer	cd_name	catalog
Talking Heads	Speaking in Tongues	2530154
Talking Heads	Little Creatures	253052
Talking Heads	Stop Making Sense	759925186
Waits, Tom	Frank's Wild Years	756790522
Wang Chung	Points on the Curve	4004-2

publishers

pub_name	performer
Geffen	Wang Chung
Island	Waits, Tom
Warner	Talking Heads

Chapter 4 described various operations on relations, including the join. Joins are performed with the select statement. The following select statement will join the two relations cd and publishers. Each tuple from the cd relation will be matched with a tuple from the publisher relation

```
select *
    from cd, publishers
    where cd.performer = publishers.performer
```

This produces an active set of tuples containing one tuple for each of the cds found in the cd relation. Each tuple in the active set contains each of the attributes found in both relations. The active set returned by this select statement will look like this

performer	cd_name	catalog	pub_name	performer
Talking Heads	Speaking in Tongues	2530154	Warner	Talking Heads
Talking Heads	Little Creatures	253052	Warner	Talking Heads
Talking Heads	Stop Making Sense	759925186	Warner	Talking Heads
Waits, Tom	Frank's Wild Years	756790522	Island	Waits, Tom
Wang Chung	Points on the Curve	40040-2	Geffen	Wang Chung

In this example, the two relations are joined on the `performer` attribute. Each tuple in the `cd` relation is joined to a tuple in the `publishers` relation based on a match of the attribute performer.

Note that the `performer` attribute appears twice in each tuple in the active set. Once where it is drawn from the `Cd` relation and again where it is drawn from the `publishers` relation. This is because all attributes were selected with the `select *` statement.

The duplicate performer name can be eliminated from the working set by a projection with the query

```
select cd.performer, cd_name, catalog, pub_name
  from cd, publishers
  where cd.performer = publishers.performer
```

Here the attributes to be included in the working set are specified by name. Note that the performer attribute must be qualified to show which attribute it is drawn from. This query will result in a working set that looks like this

```
performer     cd_name                  catalog    pub_name
Talking Heads Speaking in Tongues      2530154    Warner
Talking Heads Little Creatures         253052     Warner
Talking Heads Stop Making Sense        759925186  Warner
Waits, Tom    Frank's Wild Years       756790522  Island
Wang Chung    Points on the Curve      40040-2    Geffen
```

The active set can also be restricted with a selection in the where clause of the `select` statement.

```
select cd.performer, cd_name, catalog, pub_name
  from cd, publishers
  where cd.performer = publishers.performer
    and cd.performer = "Talking Heads"
```

This query produces the following active set

```
performer      cd_name                    catalog    pub_name performer
Talking Heads Speaking in Tongues   2530154    Warner   Talking Heads
Talking Heads Little Creatures      253052     Warner   Talking Heads
Talking Heads Stop Making Sense     759925186 Warner   Talking Heads
```

More than two tuples can be joined.

```
select *
  from r1, r2, r3
  where r1.att1= r2.att1 and r2.attb=r3.attb
```

This is an extended join. It is extended because it joins more than two relations. In this example, the active set produced by the query will contain all the tuples of each of the three relations wherever there is a match on both the keys. There will be a tuple in the working set wherever r1.att1 = r2.att1 and r2.attb = r3.attb.

OUTER JOINS WITH THE SELECT STATEMENT

The music database is shown below again, with a small change

In this example, we have removed the tuple for Tom Waits from the publishers relation. Here again is a query that joins the two relations

```
select cd.performer, cd_name, catalog, pub_name
  from cd, publishers
  where cd.performer = publishers.performer
```

The active set returned by this query will not include a tuple for Tom Waits

```
performer      cd_name                   catalog    pub_name
Talking Heads Speaking in Tongues   2530154    Warner
Talking Heads Little Creatures      253052     Warner
Talking Heads Stop Making Sense     759925186 Warner
Wang Chung     Points on the Curve  40040-2    Geffen
```

Music Database

cd

performer	cd-Name	catalog
Talking Heads	Speaking in Tongues	2530154
Talking Heads	Little Creatures	253052
Talking Heads	Stop Making Sense	759925186
Waits, Tom	Frank's Wild Years	756790522
Wang Chung	Points on the Curve	4004-2

publishers

pub_name	performer
Geffen	Wang Chung
Warner	Talking Heads

The outer join can be used to assure that a tuple will appear in the working set for every attribute found in the cd relation.

```
select cd.performer, cd_name, catalog, pub_name
  from cd, outer publishers
  where cd.performer = publishers.performer
```

The outer join will produce a tuple in the working set for every tuple in the cd relation. Note that no publisher name is available for the Waits tuple in the active set produced by this join

performer	cd_name	catalog	pub_name
Talking Heads	Speaking in Tongues	2530154	Warner
Talking Heads	Little Creatures	253052	Warner
Talking Heads	Stop Making Sense	759925186	Warner
Waits, Tom	Frank's Wild Years	756790522	
Wang Chung	Points on the Curve	40040-2	Geffen

The query for an outer join can be restricted only with attributes found in the first, primary, relation. The same restriction used before will still work with an outer join

```
select cd.performer, cd_name, catalog, pub_name
  from cd, publishers
  where cd.performer = publishers.performer
    and cd.performer = "Talking Heads"
```

Since selections can only be restricted with Boolean expressions about attributes in the primary relation, in this following example, the expression and publishers.performer = "Talking Heads" has no effect. The active set returned by this query contain five tuples, one for each tuple found in the cd relation.

```
select cd.performer, cd_name, catalog, pub_name
  from cd, publishers
  where cd.performer = publishers.performer
    and cd.performer = "Talking Heads"
```

Note that the query will not fail, the selection on the second relation is just ignored.

Outer joins can also be extended to more than two relations.

```
select *
    from r1, outer r2, outer r3
    where r1.a1=r2.a1 and r2.a2=r3.a2
```

In an extended outer join, restrictions can still only be specified on attributes found in the first, primary relation. In this example Boolean expressions restricting the query will only be performed on attributes found in relation r1.

The precedence of outer joins can be set by as follows

```
select *
    from r1, outer (r2, outer r3)
    where r1.a1=r2.a1 and r2.a2=r3.a2
```

This statement will join r2 with r3. Then the result of this outer product will be joined to r1.

ADDING DATA TO A DATABASE

Data can be added to a relation with the insert statement. where the contents of the record cd_record is added to the cd relation

```
database music
main
define
  cd_record like cd.*
  let cd_record.performer = "Basha"
  let cd_record.cd_name = "Time and Tide"
   let cd_record.catalog = "7464-407767"
  insert into cd values (cd_record.*)
end main
```

After this insertion, the cd relation will look like this

```
performer      cd_name               catalog

Talking Heads  Speaking in Tongues   2530154

Talking Heads  Little Creatures      253052

Talking Heads  Stop Making Sense     759925186

Wang Chung     Points on the Curve   40040-2

Basha          Time and Tide         7464-40767
```

Here is another format for the insert statement. In this example, each of the data values is given explicitly

```
database music
main
  insert into cd
    values("Basha","Time and Tide","7464-407767")
end main
```

Note there must be a data value for each attribute in the table. Note also the column names shown in the first example are optional. If no column names are given, values are entered into the tuple in the order they appear. The first value goes in the first attribute, the second value in the second attribute, and so on.

Variable and constant values can also be intermixed

```
insert into customer values
  (0, f_name, l_name, comp, addr1,
    addr2, "Palo Alto", "CA", zip, phone)
```

The values in an insert statement do not have to be of the same type as the attributes they will be inserted into. 4GL will automatically convert the specified data to the appropriate type if it is at all possible.

Only char data can be inserted into an attribute of type char. A character string representing a number will be converted to a number for insertion into an attribute of numeric type. Note that dates and character strings expressed as constants must be enclosed in quotes as shown in the example above.

SERIAL NUMBERS

There may be one serial field in any relation. Here is the cd relation with a new serial field added

```
ser_no    performer     cd_name                catalog
     1    Talking Heads Speaking in Tongues    2530154
     2    Talking Heads Little Creatures       253052
     3    Talking Heads Stop Making Sense      759925186
     4    Wang Chung    Points on the Curve    40040-2
     5    Waits, Tom    Frank's Wild Years     756790522
```

A serial field must be added in two steps. First add a new integer field, then change the type of the field from integer to serial

```
alter table cd
  add(ser_no integer before performer)
alter table cd
  modify(ser_no serial)
```

The newly added attribute will be null in each tuple. The records must each be updated to contain a serial value. Updating is covered in the section after next.

When adding a new tuple to a relation you can specify a serial number explicitly.

```
database music
main
define
  cd_record like cd.*
  let ser_no = 6
  let cd_record.performer = "Basha"
  let cd_record.cd_name = "Time and Tide"
  let cd_record.catalog = "7464-407767"
  insert into cd values (cd_record.*)
end main
```

In this example a new record is added with a serial number of 6. An attempt to add a record with a serial number that is already in use will fail. The successful or unsuccessful completion of the insertion can be determined with a value returned in the built-in record sqlca.

```
database music
main
define
  cd_record record like cd.*
  let ser_no = 6
  let cd_record.performer = "Basha"
  let cd_record.cd_name = "Time and Tide"
  let cd_record.catalog = "7464-407767"
  insert into cd values (cd_record.*)
```

```
  if sqlca.sqlcode > 0 then
    display "No record added, there is a problem."
  else
    display "A new record has been added."
  end if
end main
```

The serial number can be generated automatically. Assign the value zero to the serial field in the tuple to be added. When the tuple is added to the relation, the next available serial number in order will be automatically generated

```
database music
main
define
  cd_record record like cd.*
  let ser_no = 0
  let cd_record.performer = "Basha"
  let cd_record.cd_name = "Time and Tide"
  let cd_record.catalog = "7464-407767"
  insert into cd values (cd_record.*)
end main
```

The value of the generated serial number is returned in the built-in record sqlca. which displays the value of the automatically generated serial number

```
database music
main
define
  cd_record record like cd.*
  let ser_no = 0
  let cd_record.performer = "Basha"
  let cd_record.cd_name = "Time and Tide"
  let cd_record.catalog = "7464-407767"
  insert into cd values (cd_record.*)
  display "Ser #= ", sqlca.sqlerrd[2]
end main
```

DELETING DATA FROM A DATABASE

One or more records can be removed from a relation with the delete statement.

```
delete from items where order_num = onum
```

This statement will remove any tuple in the items relation where the order number is equal to the value held in the variable onum.

If a cursor is in use, open, and pointing to a tuple, that tuple can be deleted with a delete statement that has a current of clause. This statement will delete whichever tuple is currently selected by an open cursor

```
delete from orders
   where current of query_cursor
```

To delete the current tuple by using a current of clause with a delete statement, the opened cursor must have been declared with a for update clause

```
declare c_order cursor for
   select * from orders
   for update
```

The current of clause can't be used in a delete statement to delete tuples selected with a scrolling cursor.

CHANGING DATA IN A DATABASE

One or more tuples in a relation can be changed with the update statement. This example will update every tuple in a relation named stock where the attribute manu_code has the value HRO. If only one record matches the value HRO, then only one record will be updated.

```
update stock
  set unit_price =  unit_price * 1.04
  where manu_ code = "HRO"
```

After this statement, the value of the unit_price for each tuple
where the manu_code is HRO will be increased by 1.04.

Explicit values can be used in an update

```
update customer
  set (fname, company, address2) =
    ("Marie", "Marie's Sports",
     "P.O. BOx 3621")
    where customer_num = 103
```

The number of attributes that are to be changed must be the same
as the number of values that are given for the changes.

If a nonscrolling cursor was declared for update and opened, and
it is pointing to a tuple, the current record can be updated. The
update statement must include a current of clause

```
update stock
  set unit_price = 100
  current of c_stock
```

Attributes containing serial numbers can't be updated. To update
a tuple, and exclude the serial number, use the following form of
the update statement

```
update customer
  set [customer.]* = cust_record.*
```

By placing the relation name within brackets, the serial number
will be excluded from the update.

AGGREGATE FUNCTIONS

Several functions are available for use within a `select` statement. These functions will allow calculations to be performed on the rows returned by a `select` statement. Aggregate functions can return more than one tuple. When this happens a scrolling cursor must be used to manipulate the returned tuples.

Count

The `count` function will count each of the rows selected by a query

```
database stores
main
define n_states smallint
  select count(*) into n_states from state
  display "Number os states in database  ", n_states
end
```

This program will display the message `Number of states in database = 50`. Please note that the count function must always have the form `count(*)`. The count function will not take an attribute, or a list of attributes, as an argument.

Average

The arithmetic mean is computed with the `average` function

```
database stores
main
define avg_chg money
  select average(ship_charge)
    into avg_chg from orders
  display "Average shipping charge:", avg_charge
end
```

This program will display the message Average shipping
charge $13.13.

Max

The maximum value for an attribute found in the tuples returned
by a query is available with the max function. Note that the max
function can return multiple tuples

```
select max( ship_charge )
   into max_charge from orders
```

Min

The minimum function will return the lowest value for the
specified attribute found in those tuples returned by a query. Note
that the min function can return multiple tuples, in which case a
scrolling cursor must be used

```
select min( ship_charge )
   into min_charge from orders
```

Sum

The sum of all the values returned by a query for a single attribute
can be found with the sum function

```
select sum( ship_charge )
   into ship_charge from orders
```

DATE FUNCTIONS

Functions which manipulate dates can be used anywhere in a
select statement that a constant can be used.

Date

The date function converts the expression it is called with to a value of type date.

```
database stores
main
define
  r_orders record like orders.*
  select * into r_orders
    from orders
    where order_date = date ("01/20/86")
  if status =  notfound then
    display "no record found"
  else
    display r_orders.order_date, r_orders.order_num
  end if
end main
```

This program will display the following result

```
01/20/1986      1001
```

Day

The day function accepts an expression of type date. It returns the day of the month as a value between 1 and 31.

```
database stores
main
define
  r_order_num like orders.order_num,
  day_number integer
  select order_num, day(order_date)
    into r_order_num, day_number
    from orders
    where order_date = date ("01/20/1986")
  if status = notfound then
    display "No records found"
```

```
   else
     display r_order_num, day_number
   end if
end main
```

This program will display the following results

```
1001    20
```

Month

The month function takes a value of type date and returns a value of type integer. The value returned is an integer between one and twelve. One is returned for the month of January. Twelve is returned for the month of December, and so on.

```
database stores
main
define
  r_order_num like orders.order_num,
  r_month integer
  select order_num, month(order_date)
    into r_order_num, r_month
    from orders
    where order_date = date ("01/20/1986")
  if status = notfound then
    display "records found"
  else
    display r_order_num, r_month
  end if
end main
```

Year

The year function takes as an argument a value of type date. It returns an integer value equal to the year.

```
year(r_date)
```

would return the integer value 1986 if the date held in the variable r_date were 01/22/1986.

Mdy

The mdy function takes three integer values as arguments. These represent a month, day and year. It converts the three numbers to a date and returns the date as a value of type date.

The value of the year must be large enough to indicate the full year, 1986. The value 86 will be converted to a date in the first century.

```
database stores
main
define
  r_order_num like orders.order_num,
  day_number integer
  select order_num, day(order_date)
    into r_order_num, day_number
    from orders
    where order_date = mdy(1,20,1986)
  if status = notfound then
    display "No records found"
  else
    display r_order_num, day_number
  end if
end main
```

Any expression which results in an integer value, or any variable of type integer can be used as an argument to the mdy function

```
        mdy( 1,2*5*2,year )
```

Weekday

The weekday function takes an argument of type date. It returns a number between zero and six. This number passed to the function is an integer representing the day of the week where Sunday is represented by zero and Saturday is represented by six. drawn from the Informix-4GL manual

```
select order_num, weekday(order_date) from orders
```

PERMISSIONS

The creator of the database is known as the database administrator (DBA.) When a database is created, only the DBA is
allowed permission to access that database. Other users must be
given permission to connect to the database. Only the DBA can
grant this connect privilege. Other users can be authorized to have
DBA permissions as shown below.

When a database is first created, only the DBA has permission to
create or drop relations or to add or drop indexes. Users given the
resource permission can also make these changes to the
database.

Access to a database, a relation within a database, or in some cases
an attribute within a relation can be restricted to certain named
users. This is shown in the following examples.

Database Access

This statement will allow free access to the music database to all
users. After this statement, all users have DBA, connect and
resource privileges. This statement in effect removes all restrictions on database access for all users.

```
grant all to public
```

All restrictions can be lifted for a certain group of users with a
statement like

```
grant all to joe, mary
```

Table Access

Permission to access a database can be restricted to certain relations. The `alter` permission allows a user to add or delete columns or to modify the data type of a column

```
grant alter on cd to sam
```

Permission to delete rows is given like this

```
grant delete on cd to public
```

Permission to add or delete an index is given as

```
grant index on cd to joe, sally
```

Permission to insert rows into a relation is granted with

```
grant insert on cd to public
```

Users can be authorized to access certain attributes within a relation for reading data

```
grant select (fname, lname, company, city)
    on customer to public
```

Users can be allowed to change the values of certain attributes

```
grant update (fname, lname, company, city)
    on customer to sam, paul
```

REVOKING PERMISSIONS

Permissions can be revoked with the `revoke permission` statement. The following statement will revoke all permissions for the relation `orders`

```
revoke all on orders from public
```

This statement will revoke permission for John and Mary to update or delete in the relation `customer`

```
revoke delete, update on customer from john, mary
```

This will revoke connect permission to an entire database for Mary and John

```
        revoke connect from mary, john
```

LOCKING AND UNLOCKING A RELATION

A user can lock a relation. When a relation is locked, no other users can access it. This prevents conflicting operations on the same data. The following will lock the table for exclusive use by the current user

```
        lock table cd in exclusive mode
```

No other users can access data in the locked `cd` relation. The relation is locked until the `unlock` statement is executed

```
        unlock table cd
```

The relation can be locked in either of two modes, shared or exclusive

```
        lock table cd in exclusive mode
        lock table cd in share mode
```

A relation locked in exclusive mode can not be accessed in any fashion by other users. Other users can not read data held in the relation or write data to the relation.

A relation locked in share mode can be read by other users while it is locked. It can not be updated or changed by other users. No records can be added to or deleted from a relation locked in share mode.

Table level locking should be used with caution. Whenever possible, use row level locking which is described in the following section.

Statements which change the format of a relation, like alter table and create index automatically lock the entire table during their operation.

LOCKING AND UNLOCKING A ROW

Informix-4GL locks a row when an update or fetch statement is executed and the cursor was declared with the for update clause. Each row is locked before being changed and then immediately unlocked.

SETTING THE LOCK MODE TO WAIT

A program which attempts to access a relation locked by another program will fail. This can be changed with the set lock mode statement

```
set lock mode to wait
set lock mode to not wait
```

If the lock mode is set to wait, the second program will wait until the table is unlocked instead of failing. This feature is not supported on all systems, however. There are some operating systems which do not support record level locking.

Be careful. If the first calling program locks the table and then fails, the locked record may never become available. In this case the second program will wait for the record to unlock forever. This is called a deadly embrace.

12

Flow of Control, Scope of Control

As briefly described in chapter seven, a 4GL program can contain several different modules. This chapter describes how to transfer control between these program modules. This chapter also describes how to change the flow of control within an individual module.

In every 4GL program there must be a main program. In addition, there may be a global data area. There may also be one or more functions and one or more reports.

Here is a 4GL program that counts the number of records in the cd relation of the music database. This program has a globals section, a main program and two functions

```
database music
globals
define
  r_tbl array[200] of record like cd.*,
  record_length smallint
end globals
#——————————————————--
# main
#——————————————————--
main
  let record_length = 200
  call clear_r_tbl()
  call select_records()
```

```
end main
#----------------------------------
#  select records from database
#----------------------------------
function select_records()
  define
  c_recs smallint
  declare c_tbl scroll cursor for
    select * from cd
  let c_recs = 1
  foreach c_tbl into r_tbl[c_recs].*
    let c_recs = c_recs + 1
  end foreach
    let c_recs = c_recs - 1
  if c_recs  0 then
    message "Records found that match query ",
c_recs
    sleep 2
  else
    message "No records found"
    sleep 2
  end if
end function


#----------------------------------
# Initialize array of records to null
#----------------------------------
function clear_r_tbl()
  define counter smallint
  for counter = 1 to record_length
    initialize r_tbl[counter].* to null
  end for
  return
end function
```

Point to a Database

The program starts with the statement database music. This points to the music database for any data definitions that follow. The running program will also use the music database for data access.

Global Data

The globals section contains an array of records called r_tbl. Each record is like the cd relation. Each record contains a field for each attribute found in the cd relation. The globals section also contains a single variable called record_length. This variable will be used to hold a value giving the length of the r_tbl record. I selected the name r_tbl with the prefix r_ to indicate that this variable is a record. This is nice but not mandatory.

Any data defined in the global area of the program is usable anywhere else in the program that follows. Both the record r_tbl and the variable record_length can be accessed from any of the other routines, either the main program or any function (or report if there was a report). The main program and both functions in the example program can access values held in r_tbl and record_length.

Main Program

The main program follows the globals section. It first initializes the record_length variable to the value of 200. The record length is held as in a variable so that it can be easily changed in one location. This makes it easier to change the record length throughout the program when the size of the record needs to be changed. This is easier than searching for and replacing the number 200 in a variety of locations. If the length of the record is increased, for example, just one change is needed in the program instead of many.

CALLING A FUNCTION OR REPORT

A main program can call a function or report into action. A function can call other functions. These functions can call still other functions. A function can call a report, a report can call functions. This process of one routine calling another routine is called transfer of control

In the example, the main program calls the function clear_r_tbl with the statement call clear_r_tbl( ). This statement causes control to be passed to the function clear_r_tbl. The function clear_r_tbl can be seen lower down in the example. The path that the running program takes from one routine to another, and back again, is called flow of control.

Executable Statements

Because of the function call, the next statement executed is the first executable statement found in the function clear_r_tbl.

The very first statement in this function clear_r_tbl defines a variable named counter which is a smallint. This variable will be used to point to each array element in turn.

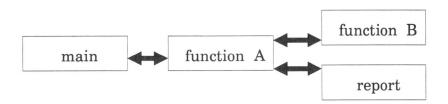

Note that the variable counter is created when the program is compiled. The definition of any data occurs when the program is compiled into a form that can be run. The space for the variable is reserved, by name, during the process of compilation.

When the program is run, the first executable statement of the function `clear_r_tbl` is

```
for counter = 1 to record_length
```

The For Statement

The `for` statement will execute all the statements found between itself and the later `end for` statement a number of times. A `for` statement has a beginning and an end

```
for ...
end for
```

All the statements between the beginning and end of the `for` statement will be executed some specified number of times. In this example, the `for` statement will be executed 200 times. The value of the variable `counterr` will start at one. The `for` statement will continue to execute all the statements between the `for` and the `end for` until the value of `counter` reaches the value of `record_length`, which in this case is `200`.

Initialize the Array of Records

The `for` statement causes the value of `counter` to take all the values from 1 to `200`, one at a time. The statement inside the `for` loop is

```
initialize r_tbl[counter].* to null
```

This will initialize each of the array elements of `r_tbl` to `null`. Each of the attributes in each record held in each array element will be initialized to `null` by this statement.

Return to Calling Program

The `return` statement is the next to last statement found in the function `clear_r_tbl`. This statement causes the program to return to where it was called from. In this example, the function was called from the main program. So control will be returned to the main program.

The `return` statement can be used anywhere within a function or report to return control to the calling program. There can be more than one `return` statement in a function. Whichever `return` statement is executed first will cause control to return to the calling program.

```
if a_var is true then
  message "Return from first return"
  return
else
  message "Return from second return"
  return
end if
```

This has explained how control is passed from one routine to another. One routine may call another routine. The statements in the called routine are executed until a `return` or the end `function`, or end `report` statement is reached. Reaching the end of a function or report, or executing a `return` statement causes control to pass back to the calling program.

One function can call another function in the same fashion. Function `clear_r_tbl` could easily call other functions. A function called from within `clear_r_tbl` could itself call one or more other functions or reports. A report can call one or more functions, each of these could call other functions.

Functions can also call themselves. This is called recursion. While a description of recursion is beyond the scope of this book, recursion is a very useful tool in certain circumstances.

Call Another Function

Control is passed back to the main program and the `clear_r_tbl` function call. The next executable statement is `call select_records`. Control is now passed to the first executable statement in the `select_records` function.

Select Records

The function `select_records` takes each available tuple out of the `cd` relation and leaves it an array element of `r_tbl`. This function will only work if the number of records found does not exceed 200. If there are more than 200 records, the size of the array would need to be increased.

With large numbers of tuples it is better to use a scrolling cursor to bring the values found in the database into a set of program variables one tuple at a time. If there are very large numbers of tuples to be manipulated, it will be impossible to reserve enough space in an array of records to hold them all. The size of storage available to a program will vary from machine to machine. In general it is unwise to bring the values stored in more than several thousand tuples into program variables all at the same time.

Display Search Results

There is an `if` statement which is used to select one of two messages to be displayed

```
if c_recs > 0 then
   message "records found that match query ", c_recs
else
   message "No records found"
end if
```

This will cause the number of records found to be displayed on the screen. The `if` statement is described at greater length in a following section. The `message` statement is described fully in the next chapter.

Ending the Program

After the `select_records` function is complete, control is passed back to the main program. Since the call to `select_records` was the last statement in the main program, the program now ends.

It is possible to leave the main program from anywhere with the `exit program` statement. This statement can be used to stop the main program anywhere instead of having to reach the `end program` statement.

PASSING DATA TO A FUNCTION OR REPORT

One or more values can be passed to a function or report when it is called as arguments. For example

```
main
define
  var1 char(10),
  var2 integer,
  var3 money
  let var1 = "1234567890"
  let var2 = 99
  let var3 = 99.95
  # call fa with five arguments
  call fa(var1,var2,var3,"text",2*5)
end main
function fa( fv1, fv2, fv3, fv4, fv5 )
define
  fv1 char(10),
  fv2 integer,
  fv3 money,
  fv4 char(10),
  fv5 integer
    display fv1,fv2,fv3,fv4,fv5)
end function
```

Only values are passed to the called function. Two values, "text" and 2*5 are passed explicitly in this example. For the other three arguments, var1, var2, and var3, the values contained in the variables are passed to the function.

Only values are passed to a called function. In the example above, the called function can not change the values contained in the variables var1, var2 and var3. Only a variable held in global storage can be changed by two different routines. This mechanism of passing a value to a called routine, rather than a variable, is known as call by value.

Since only a value is passed to the called routine, the called routine must define a variable which can hold this value when it is received from the calling program. That is why in the example there are five arguments in the statement that defines the function

```
function fa(fv1,fv2,fv3,fv4,fv5)
   fv1 char(10),
   fv2 integer,
   fv3 money,
   fv4 char(10),
   fv5 integer
```

The variables listed in the function definition are called formal parameters. These formal parameters are used during compilation to reserve space for the values that will be passed to the function by the running program.

RETURNING DATA FROM A FUNCTION

A function can return one or more values to the calling program.

```
main
define
   var1, var2 char(10)
   let var1 = "            "
   let var2 = "            "
```

```
  call f_demo() returning var1, var2
  display var1, var2
end main
function f_demo()
define
  fvar1, fvar2 char(10)
  let fvar1 = "returned"
  let fvar2 = "from f_demo"
  return fvar1, fvar2
end function
```

In this example, the function returns two values, held in fvar1 and fvar2, to the main program. Note that here again only values are passed between modules. The function can not alter the value of any variables defined in the main program. The main program can not alter the values of any variables defined in the function.

There is no mechanism for returning values from a report routine.

FLOW OF CONTROL IN A MODULE

The preceding sections have shown how control can flow between routines. The course of execution within a routine can also be changed with various statements. These statements, goto, if, for, while, case and foreach are described in the following sections .

GOTO

The goto statement transfers control from the goto statement to another labeled statement

```
main
  goto label2
label label1: display "label one reached"
label label2: display label two reached
```

In this example, when the goto statement is executed control of the running program is transferred to the statement with the label label2. When this program is run, only the following will be displayed: Label two reached.

Now that you know what the goto does, forget about it. Except under the most rare conditions the goto is never used in a well written program.

Why? A goto statement can make it very difficult to discern the flow of control within a routine. Other control statements can effect program flow of control as needed and result in much more orderly and well written programs.

IF

The if statement selects between two alternatives

```
if statement_1 then
   do this
else
   do this instead
end if
```

Statement_1 is any expression which results in a Boolean value of true or false. That is, statement_1 should result in a value of true (1), or false (zero.)

```
main
define
   var1 integer
   let var1 = true
   if var1 then
     display "var one was true"
   end if
#
   if var1 then
     display "two way if"
```

```
      else
        display "didn't get here"
      end if
end main
```

The first `if` statement in the example is a one-way `if` statement. If `var1` is true, then the message `var1 was true` is displayed when the program is run.

The second `if` statement selects between one of two alternatives. If `var1` is `true`, the message `two way if` is displayed when the program is run. If `var1` is set to `false`, the message `didn't get here` is displayed when the program is run.

Any legal Boolean expression, as described in chapter 9, can be used in an if statement to determine the flow of control of the running program.

```
if b > (b - c - d + (a-4)*5) then do this end if

if a is true and b is false then do this end if
```

Combining if Statements

If statements can be nested.

```
main
define
  var1, var2 integer
  let var1 = true
  let var2 = true
  if var1 then
    if var2 then
      display "var one and two were true."
    end if
  end if
end main
```

This program, when run, will display the message var one and two were true.

Nested if statements can also be used to select from a number of choices, one after the other

```
main
define
  var1, var2, var3 integer
  let var1 = false
  let var2 = false
  let var3 = true
  if var1 then
    display "var one was true"
  else
    if var2 then
      display "var two was true."
  else
    if var3 then
      display "only var3 was true."
  end if
  end if
  end if
end main
```

If var1 is true, only the first statement will be printed and the if statement will end. If var1 is false, but var2 is true, then the second message is displayed and the if statement ends. If var1 and var2 are false, but var3 is true, only the last message is displayed.

FOR

The for statement has a beginning and an end. All the statements between the beginning and end of the for statement are executed some number of times based on the variables which control the statement.

```
main
define
  var1, var2, var3 integer
  let var2 = 1
  let var3 = 10
  for var1 = var2 to var3
    display "var1 = ", var1
  end for
end main
```

This example will display the message ten times, once for each value of var1. The if statement starts by assigning the value 1 to the variable var1. Then the message is displayed for the first time. When the end for statement is reached, the value of var1 is compared to the value of var3. If var1 is less than var3, var1 is increased by 1 and the statements contained within the for statement are executed again.

The increment can be something other than one. This program will display only the even numbers from two to ten

```
main
define
  var1, var2, var3, var4 integer
  let var2 = 2
  let var3 = 10
  let var4 = 2
  for var1 = var2 to var3 step var4
    display "var1 = ", var1
  end for
end main
```

The increment can be given as any legal expression which results in an integer value.

```
        for var1 = var2 to var3 step ((8/4)*4)/4
```

The next alternation of the for loop can be invoked directly with the continue for statement bypassing other statements within the for loop.

```
main
define
  var1, var2, var3, var4 integer
  let var2 = 2
  let var3 = 10
  let var4 = 2
  for var1 = var2 to var3 step var4
    if var1 < 5 then continue for end if
    display "var1 = ", var1
  end for
end main
```

In this example, the continue for statement will be invoked whenever the value of var1 is less than 5. This causes control to be passed to the end for statement, bypassing the message, until the value of var1 reaches 6. The value of var1 is incremented by 2, tested against the value of var3, and if the value of var1 is still less than the value of var3, the for statement is run again.

The for loop can be ended completely with the exit for statement

```
main
define
  var1, var2, var3, var4 integer
  let var2 = 2
  let var3 = 10
  let var4 = 2
  for var1 = var2 to var3 step var4
    if var1 > 5 then exit for end if
    display "var1 = ", var1
  end for
end main
```

In this example, the message is displayed twice for the values 2 and 4. When the `if` statement determines the value of `var1` is greater than 5, the `for` loop is stopped.

WHILE

The `while` statement has a beginning and an end. The statements between the beginning of the `while` loop and the end of the `while` loop are each executed as long as the stated condition remains true

```
main
define
   condition, var1 integer
   let var1 = 1
   let condition = true
   while condition
     let var1 = var1 + 1
     if var1 > 5 then let condition = false end if
     display "var1 = ", var1
   end while
end main
```

This example will display the message six times. When `var1` is incremented to contain a value of 6, the variable `condition` is set to `false`. The variable `condition` is examined each time the end `while` statement is reached. If the value of the condition is `true`, the while loop is executed again. If, at the end of the while loop, the condition has become `false`, control passes to the next statement following the end `while` statement.

As with the for loop, execution of the `while` statement can be controlled with the `continue while` and `exit while` statements

```
main
define
   condition, var1 integer
   let var1 = 1
```

```
   let condition = true
   while condition
     if var1 < 5 then continue while end if
     let var1 = var1 + 1
     if var1 > 5 then let condition = false end if
     display "var1 = ", var1
   end while
end main
```

This example will skip from the statement if var1 < 5 . . . to the end of the while loop until the value of var1 is equal to 5.

```
main
define
   condition, var1 integer
   let var1 = 1
   let condition = true
   while condition
     if var1 > 7 then exit while end if
     let var1 = var1 + 1
     if var1 > 5 then let condition = false end if
     display "var1 = ", var1
   end while
end main
```

This while loop will end when the value of var1 reaches 7.

CASE

The case statement executes one group of statements selected from several groups of statements based on a Boolean selector statement.

```
main
define
   selector, dummy integer
   let selector = 2
```

```
    case
      when selector = 1
        display "selector = 1"
        let dummy =   1
      when selector = 2
        display "selector = 2"
        let dummy = 2
      when selector = 3
        display "selector = 3"
        let dummy = 3
    end case
end main
```

Each of the when clauses in a case statement is tried in turn. When the Boolean expression associated with a when clause evaluates to true, the statements associated with that when clause are executed.

In the example, the first Boolean expression, selector = 1, evaluates to a value of false. Since the Boolean selector expression evaluates to false, the two following statements associated with this where clause are skipped.

The Boolean expression associated with the second when clause, selector = 2, evaluates to true. The two following statements are executed and the message selector = 2 is displayed.

When a when clause has been successfully executed, control passes to the end while statement. After a when clause is executed, no other when clauses are evaluated and the case statement is ended. If there were two when clauses in a case statement which would evaluate to true at run-time, only the first will be executed

```
main
define
  selector, dummy integer
  let selector = 2
  case
    when selector = 1
```

```
        display "selector = 1"
        let dummy =   1
    when selector = 2
        display "selector = 2"
        let dummy = 2
    when selector = 2 # This will never execute!
        display "selector = 2"
        let dummy = 3
  end case
end main
```

When no Clause is True

Often, none of the where clauses in a case statement will evaluate
to true. It is good programming practice to be prepared for this by
using the otherwise clause

```
main
define
   selector, dummy integer
   let selector = 4
   case
     when selector = 1
       display "selector = 1"
       let dummy =   1
     when selector = 2
       display "selector = 2"
       let dummy = 2
     when selector = 2 # This will never execute!
       display "selector = 2"
       let dummy = 3
     otherwise
       display "Incorrect selector"
       let dummy = false
   end case
end main
```

Selectors That are not Boolean Expressions

An expression can be used in the case definition to change the
type of the selector from Boolean to any other type. When a
different type of selector is used, each of the expressions following
a when clause must evaluate to this type. Here is an example where
the selection is based on a character type variable

```
main
define
   selector char(2)
   let selector = "C"
   case (selector) #selector is the variable name
     when "A"
       display "selector = A"
     when "B"
       display "selector = B"
     when "C"
       display "selector = C"
     otherwise
       display "Incorrect selector"
   end case
end main
```

This example will display the message Selector = C when run.

Exit Case

The exit case clause can be used to exit a case statement at any
time. An exit case clause is implied with each when clause, but
may be written explicitly

```
   case (selector)
     when "A"
       if condition then exit case end if
       display "selector = A"
       exit case
     when "B"
       display "selector = B"
```

```
   otherwise
      display "Incorrect selector"
   end case
```

FOREACH

The foreach statement has been described in chapter 11. The foreach statement is used to move a cursor through an active set of tuples selected from a database. The foreach statement will open a cursor, move the cursor to each selected tuple, one after the other, and then close the cursor

```
foreach cursor-name into variable-list
   (do these statements)
end foreach
```

A with the while and for statements, the flow of control within a foreach statement can be modified with the exit foreach and continue foreach statements.

The exit foreach statement will cause control to be passed to the end foreach statement where the open cursor will be closed and control is passed to the following statements.

The continue foreach causes control to be passed to the end foreach statement. If there are remaining tuples in the active set, the foreach loop is executed again. If there are no more tuples to be found in the active set, the cursor is closed and control is passed to the next statement following the end foreach statement

```
foreach cursor_name into variable_list
   if condition then exit foreach end if
   if condition then continue foreach end if
end foreach
```

ERROR PROCESSING

There are sometimes errors during database access. If an error occurs, the built-in variable status will be set to some value less than zero (status < 0). An if statement can test for this condition

```
if status < 0 then
    error processing statements
end if
```

Warnings are sometimes produced during database access. , if an attribute selected from a database is truncated when it is copied to a program variable, a warning will be issued. When a warning is given, the built-in variable sqlca.sqlawarn[2] will be set to a value of W.

An if statement can detect a warning

```
if sqlca.sqlawarn[2] = "W" then
    respond to warning
else
    do this
end if
```

WHENEVER

The whenever statement can be used to process errors and warnings instead of an if statement.

```
whenever error call function_name
```

This statement will call a separate function whenever an error occurs during database access. The following statement will respond in a similar fashion to warnings generated during database access

```
whenever warning call function_name
```

Each of these statements should be used only once early on in a program. Issued once at the beginning of a main routine, they will affect the processing of errors or warnings for the rest of the program. An example of this can be seen in the Informix supplied demo program ch10when.4gl.

This statement will cause any database access errors to be ignored. It overrides a previously issued whenever error statement.

```
whenever error continue
insert into orders (order_num) values (0)
if status < 0 then
  display "Error during Insert"
end if
```

If a whenever error statement was in effect before this example an error during the insert would cause that previous whenever statement to be executed. The whenever error continue statement in the example above will cause the previously selected error processing to be turned off. This allows the if statement shown in the example to be correctly executed. Without the whenever error continue statement, the whenever error statement found earlier in the program would be executed first, then the if statement would find an error condition and also execute the display "Error during Insert" statement.

WAITING: THE SLEEP STATEMENT

A running program can be made to wait for a specified number of seconds with the sleep statement

```
        if tired then
          sleep 2
        else
          return
        end if
```

INTERRRUPTS

Two different signals, quit and interrupt, can be sent to a running program. These signals are sent when certain keys are pressed. With UNIX, for example, the quit signal is often sent by holding down the control key and pressing c. Again with UNIX, the interrupt is often sent by holding down the control key and pressing the \ key. The key sequences used to generate an interrupt or quit are different in different operating environments. Consult your system documentation or your system administrator to find the key sequences that transmit these signals on your system.

Sending either a quit or an interrupt to a running program stops that program. The program is stopped immediately no matter which statement is being executed. These signals override the normal flow of control of a running program.

The defer statement changes this. These two statements will prevent a running program from stopping when either an interrupt or quit signal is sent

```
defer interrupt
defer quit
```

The defer statements have another effect. If the defer interrupt statement has been executed, when an interrupt is received by the running program, the global variable int_flag will be set to a value other than zero. Similarly, if a running program receives a quit signal when a defer quit statement has been previously executed, the quit signal will not stop the running program and the variable quit_flag will be set to a nonzero value. Here is a program which services the interrupt signal

```
main
  define
    end_flag char(1)
  defer interrupt
  while true
    if int_flag <>  0 then
      message "Program was interrupted"
      let int_flag = 0
      prompt "Stop (y/n) " for end_flag
      if end_flag = "y" or end_flag = "Y" then
        exit while
      end if
    end if
  end while
end main
```

Note that the variable int_flag must be reset to zero by the program in order for the program to be ready to service another interrupt. It is the responsibility of the programmer to assure that the variable int_flag is re-set to zero after it has been set by an interrupt to a value other than zero.

13

Displaying Data

This chapter describes how data is displayed on-screen. The first sections of the chapter describes how simple data is displayed to the screen, or accepted from the user. Later sections of the chapter describe how a screen form is built and managed. The final section of the chapter describes the use of windows for the display of data or forms.

DISPLAY

The `display` statement manages the presentation of single lines of data to the screen. The `display` statement can present variable and literal information.

```
display Variable one has a value of: , var1
```

This statement displays the message `Variable one has a value of`, and the value held in `var1` on the first available screen line. For example, if `var1` holds a value of 100 this will display

```
Variable one has a value of:        100
```

Each succeeding display statement will print on the next available screen line. For example, these two statements will produce two separate lines on the display

```
display "message one"
display "message two"
```

```
message one
message two
```

The section on character expressions in chapter nine shows how strings can be manipulated with operations like clipping and concatenation. Each of these can be used in a display statement.

```
display "12345      " clipped, "6789"
```

will display 123456789 on the display screen. The first character string is clipped of trailing blanks. This resulting clipped string is concatenated with the second string and displayed on screen.

An optional at clause cause can be used to display data at a specified location

```
display "Message" at 3,4
```

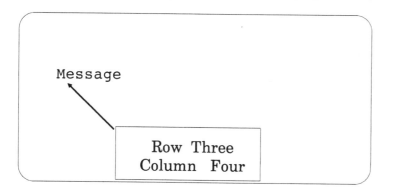

This statement will display the word Message at the third row and fourth column of the display screen as shown in the following figure

CHANGING THE DISPLAY ATTRIBUTES

The display attributes of the information presented with a display statement can be changed. Not all attributes are available on all terminals. Here is a list of the possible display attributes

NAME	EFFECT
reverse	video
underline	underlined
bold	brighter than normal
normal	intensity
invisible	not displayed at all
blink	blinks on and off, use sparingly

With a color display, various colors can be selected. They are white, yellow, magenta, cyan, green, blue and black.

that displays data in red and in reverse video

```
display "Sample Message" attribute(reverse, red)
```

These same attributes can be used with the `error` and `message` statements that are described in sections below.

PROMPTING THE USER

```
Please enter a number from one to ten:




```

The `prompt` statement can solicit a response from the user.

```
main
define
   var1 integer
prompt "Please enter a number from one to ten ",
var1
end main
```

This will present the message on screen and wait for a response from the user

THE OPTIONS STATEMENT

There is a separate `options` statement that changes the position where prompts will appear on screen. Unlike the `display` statement, there is no optional `at` clause that can be used to determine where a prompt is displayed. where the `options` statement is used to set the prompt line to the 24th screen line

```
main
define
  var1 integer
  options
    prompt line 24
  prompt "enter a number:" for var1
  prompt "enter a second number" for var1
end main
```

Each of the prompts displayed by this example will appear on the 24th screen line. The display attributes of a `prompt` statement cannot be changed with an `attributes` clause. There is no attributes clause in the `prompt` statement.

Note that the `prompt` statement will not perform any error checking on data typed in by the user. If the user types a letter in response to the prompt in the above example, the program will fail because it expects an integer value. To overcome this problem, accept all prompts as character strings and then convert them with assignment statements

```
main
define
  var1 char(20),
  var2 integer
  options
    prompt line 24
  prompt "enter a number" for var1
  let var2 = var1
```

```
    display "converted value: ",var2 at 1,1
end main
```

This will not prevent all errors. The string functions described in chapter nine can be used to examine the contents of the string input by the user. If any characters like letters appear in the string the conversion to an integer can be skipped.

The following sections on screen forms present a better mechanism for testing input from the user for correctness.

MESSAGES AND ERROR MESSAGES

Two other output statements are available, one for displaying messages and another for displaying error messages. As with the prompt statement, the options statement can specify the line that each of these messages is displayed on.

Each of these statements displays a list of constants or variables. All the attributes listed above can be used. Error messages are displayed in reverse video as a matter of course

```
main
define
  var1 char(30),
  var2 integer
  options
    prompt line 1,
    message line 22,
    error line 21
  let var1 = "This is a message"
  prompt "Enter a number from 1 to 10:" for var1
  message "--", var1, "--" attribute(red)
  let var1 = "This is an error message"
  error "***", var1, "***"
  prompt "Enter a number from 1 t0 10:" for var1
end main
```

This program displays each of the two prompts on the first line of the screen. The error message is displayed in reverse video on line 21 of the screen. The message shows at line 22 of the display. The error message is automatically cleared at the next user keystroke.

CLEARING THE SCREEN

All displayed data can be cleared from the screen with the clear screen statement

```
main
   display "Here is a message"
   clear screen
end main
```

RING MENUS

Chapter eight described how to run Informix-4GL. The various operations available were selected from ring menus. Here is an example of a ring menu

```
OPTIONS: Query  Display  Modify  Exit
Select Records
```

Four choices are available. Each time the space bar is pressed, the next choice is highlighted. The Enter key selects the operation highlighted to be executed.

Any menu item can be executed directly by typing the first letter of the command name. For example, the Exit command is always available by typing e, or E, for exit.

After the last choice is selected with the space bar, in this case Exit, the first choice, Query, is highlighted again. This is why the menu is called a ring menu.

Here is the program that displays this ring menu

```
main
   menu "OPTIONS"
   command "Query" "Select records"
   command "Display" "Display the selected records"
   command "Modify" "Add of Change records"
   command "Exit" "Exit this menu"
   end menu
   clear screen
end main
```

Groups of statements, or calls to reports or functions, can be associated with each command.

```
main
   menu "OPTIONS"
   command "Query"
"Select records"
   command "Display" "Display the selected records"
      display "Record One"
      display "Record Two"
      call function_A()
   command "Modify" "Add of Change records"
   command "Exit" "Exit this menu"
   end menu
   clear screen
end main
function _A()
   return
end function
```

Changing the Order of Menu Selections

The next option clause of the menu statement can select which choice will be highlighted next. This changes the regular order of one item being selected after the other

```
menu "OPTIONS"
command "Query" "Select records"
  next option "Modify"
command "Display" "Display the selected records"
command "Modify" "Add of Change records"
command "Exit" "Exit this menu"
end menu
```

When this program is run, the same choices appear in the ring menu as before. If the option Q is selected, however, by typing the letter Q, or by highlighting the Q selection and pressing the Enter key, the selection Modify will be highlighted and left available for selection with the Enter key.

Continuing or Exiting a Menu

The execution of a ring menu statement is continued with the continue menu statement. The menu is exited with the exit menu statement.

```
main
  define
    c_select char(10)
  menu "OPTIONS"
  command "Query" "Select records"
  command "Display" "Display the selected records"
  command "Modify" "Add of Change records"
  command "Exit" "Exit this menu"
    clear screen
    prompt "Please enter y to exit:", for c_select
    if c_select = "Y" or c_select = "y" then
      exit menu
    else
```

```
        continue menu
      end if
    end menu
    clear screen
end main
```

SCREEN FORMS

The prompt statement presented a message on screen and allowed the user to type a response. Screen forms provide a similar, more powerful, facility.

A screen form contains screen fields where data can be displayed to the user or accepted from the user. A screen form also contains descriptive labels. of a screen form

```
              States
Abbreviation: [   ]
Name: [                    ]
```

This example has two screen fields and three labels. The fields are delimited by brackets. Under the direction of a running 4GL program, data can be displayed to either of these fields, or accepted from the user from either field.

A 4GL program starts as a series of program statements held in a file. This file is compiled into an executable program. Similarly, a form starts as a description held in a file. This description is compiled into a format that can be used by a running 4GL program

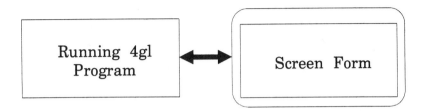

The running program can display data in each screen field. The user can also type data into any of the fields under control of the running 4GL program..

Here is the form description file used to produce the screen form shown in the example above

```
database stores
screen
{
          States
Abbreviation: [fa]
Name: [f001                        ]
}
end
tables
state
attributes
fa = state.code;
f001 = state.sname;
end
```

This form description has several parts. The first statement, database stores, identifies the database that will be used to validate the size of each of the screen fields. This statement has much the same effect as the database statement in a 4GL program.

The contents of the form, as displayed on screen, is held between the brackets

```
screen
{
        the description of the form display goes here
}
```

This description has two types of information. Literal text is typed in as it is presented on the display. For example, the label `States` is typed as it appears on-screen when the running 4GL program displays the compiled form.

Entry fields, where data can be displayed or accepted, are shown with brackets, for example `[fa]`. There is also a label, in this case `fa`, between the brackets. The brackets show the amount of space reserved for the field. The area between the two brackets is where data will be displayed or accepted when the form is displayed under the control of a running program.

The label `fa` identifies the form field. The label is used again further down in the form description to associate the display field with an attribute in a relation. In this example, the field `fa` is used to display data found in the `code` attribute of the `state` relation.

When the form is displayed, one of the fields is selected at any one time by the running 4GL program. The active field is indicated by the presence of the display-cursor. This display-cursor is usually a square block that may or may not be blinking on-and-off and which may be shown in reverse video. The cursor may just be an underline on your display, though.

The display of data, the acceptance of data, and the movement of the display-cursor from field to field is controlled by the running 4GL program. This process is described below.

The `tables` section of the form description names each of the tables that are referenced by this form. In the example, the only table referenced is the `cd` table. Forms can be used to display data from more than one relation. Forms can also have fields that are not associated with a database attribute.

BUILD AND COMPILE A SCREEN FORM

From the first 4GL or R4GL screen type `F` for form and then `N` for new.

You will be asked to name the form. Type in a name and press the `Enter` key. The development facility will automatically add the suffix `.per` to the name you have chosen. For example, if you name the form `cd` the form will be saved in the file `cd.per`. The length of the name will be limited to the number of characters allowed for your operating system, for example eight characters for DOS.

After typing the name of the form, press the `Enter` key. The text editor will open. You can now enter any screen-form statements. Save the file with your editor commands. The menu choice compile will be highlighted. Press `Enter` to compile the form. If there are errors in the form you will be given an opportunity to correct them. If there are no errors, a form file will be created. This form file will be named with the name you typed in and a `.frm` suffix. This compiled form can now be used by a running 4GL program.

Compiling from the Operating System Prompt

A file containing a form specification can be compiled from the operating system prompt with the command

```
form4gl file-name
```

where `file-name` is the name of the file containing the form specification. Note that it is not necessary to include the `.per` suffix with the file name. For example, a form specification held in

a file named `cd.per` can be compiled with the command `form4gl`
`cd`. Error messages are left in a file with the name of the form and
a `.err` suffix.

Adding an option of -v on the command line will cause the width
of form fields to be checked against the database. If any fields are
found which are not wide enough to allow the complete display of
data stored in the database, an error message is given

```
form4gl -v file-name
```

BUILDING A FORM AUTOMATICALLY

4GL or R4GL will build a form for you, automatically. From the
`Form` menu, type G for generate.. You will be prompted for the name
of the form. Type in the name you would like and press `Enter`. A
list of the tables in the selected database is shown on screen. For
the stores database, the list looks like this illustration.

```
customer
items
manufact
orders
state
stock
syscolatt
```

A form can be built automatically for one or more tables in a
database. This example shows how to build a form used with a
single relation.

To select the relation, type in the name of a table and press Enter, or use the cursor keys to highlight a selection and press Enter. The menu selection Table-selection-complete will be high-lighted. Press the Enter key and a form will be generated and compiled.

Here is a form generated automatically from the state relation of the stores database

```
database stores
screen
{
code              [a0]
sname             [f000                           ]
}
end
tables
state
attributes
a0 = state.code;
f000 = state.sname;
end
```

DISPLAYING A FORM FROM A PROGRAM

The compiled form can now be displayed on-screen by a running 4GL program. This program will display the form named state created in the previous example. Note the name of the screen form is given between quotes and does not include the .frm extension. Note the form name is not declared in a define   section.

```
main
   open form state from "state"
   display form state
   sleep 10
   close form state
   clear screen
end main
```

This is what the form will look like on the screen

```
code            [a0]
sname           [f000                        ]
```

The program opens the form file and displays the form for ten seconds. The form is then closed, the screen is cleared and the program ends.

DISPLAY DATA

The display statement will show variable or constant data on a screen-form.

```
database stores
main
  define
    code like state.code,
    state like state.sname
  open form state from "state"
  display form state
  let state = "California"
  let code = "CA"
  display code, state to code, sname
  sleep 10
  close form state
  clear screen
end main
```

This `display` statement shows the listed variables or constants in the named screen fields. The names of the screen fields are determined in the form specification. The variables can have any valid name. This `display` statement would also work in the above program

```
display "CA","California" to code, sname
```

Data is displayed in the order listed in the `display` statement. The order will not alter the correct positioning of data on the form. This statement will also work correctly

```
display state, code to sname, code
```

DISPLAY DATA BY NAME

If the program variables have names that are the same as the names chosen for the fields in the form specification, a shorter form of the display statement can be used. Variables can be displayed to screen fields by name. In this example, the variable names chosen in the program are identical to the names of the field in the form specification

```
database stores
main
  define
    code like state.code,
    sname like state.sname
  open form state from "state"
  display form state
  let state = "California"
  let code = "CA"
  display by name code, sname
  sleep 10
  close form state
  clear screen
end main
```

Here too, order is not important. This display statement will also work correctly

```
display by name sname, code
```

The variables are displayed in different order by this statement, but they are still displayed to the correct fields on the form.

DISPLAYING DATA WITH ATTRIBUTES

Attributes are still available when displaying data to a screen-form. For example, the display statement in the previous example can be changed to

```
display by name sname, code attribute(reverse)
```

FORMONLY FIELDS

Forms can have fields which are not associated with an attribute in the database. These are formonly fields. of a form that has a formonly field

```
database stores
screen
{
code            [a0]
sname                [f000                          ]
message         [f001                    ]
}
end
tables
state
attributes
a0 = state.code;
f000 = state.sname;
f001 = formonly.msg
end
```

Here is a sample program which will display data to the `formonly` field

```
database stores
main
  define
    code like state.code,
    sname like state.sname,
    msg char(20)
  open form state from "state"
  display form state
  let state = "California"
  let code = "CA"
  let msg = "A test message"
  display by name code, sname, msg
  sleep 10
  clear screen
end main
```

If all the fields in a form description are `formonly`, the first statement in the file must be

```
        database formonly
```

CLEARING A FORM

A form is completely cleared of any displayed data with the `clear form` statement. This program will display data, clear the form, and then display new data

```
database stores
main
  define
    code like state.code,
    sname like state.sname
  open form state from "state"
  display form state
  let state = "California"
```

```
      let code = "CA"
      display by name code, sname, msg
      sleep 2
      clear form
      let sname = "Texas"
      let code = "TX"
      display by name code, sname
      sleep 2
      close form state
      clear screen
end main
```

INPUT DATA

The user can input data into a form under the control of a running 4GL program. This program will allow the user to input a state name and state code into the state form

```
database stores
main
  define
    code like state.code,
    sname like state.sname
  options
    message line 24
  open form state from "state"
  display form state
  input code, sname from code, sname
  message "code= ", code, " sname= ", sname
  sleep 2
  close form state
  clear screen
end main
```

When this program is run, the `state` form will be displayed on the screen. The cursor will be left in the input field named `code`. The user can type up to two characters into this field. Any further characters typed by the user will be ignored.

When the user presses the `Enter` key, the cursor moves to the next field, the `sname` field. The user can type characters into this field as before, until the end of the field is reached. Characters typed by the user after the end of the field has been reached will be ignored.

The `tab` key and `back-tab` key can be used to move from field to field. Cursor keys will also move the cursor within the field, or to the next field. The `Enter` key will also move the cursor to the next screen field.

When the user presses the `Enter` key again, a message will be displayed on the 24th line of the screen echoing what was typed into the two screen fields.

The order in which fields are read by the `input` statement is determined by the order in which variables appear in the `input` statement. For example, this statement will read the state name before the state code

```
input sname, code from sname, code
```

Note that the field names must appear in the same order as the variable names. This statement will not work correctly

```
input sname, code from code, sname
```

INPUT BY NAME

If the variables in a program have names that are the same as the names of fields in a form, the fields can be read by name. The order the fields are read is the same as the order in which variables appear in the `input` statement. For example, this statement will read the state name and then the state code

```
input by name sname, code
```

ATTRIBUTES IN A FORM SPECIFICATION

Attributes can be added to a form description to control the operation of the form at run-time. For example, attributes are available to cause a field to be skipped by the input statement. Other form attributes validate data entered by the user. Attributes can provide a default value for fields. This section describes each of these attributes. Attributes are shown in the attributes section of a form specification after the field identifier for an individual field.

```
database stores
screen
{
code              [a0]
sname             [f000                         ]
}
end
tables
state
attributes
a0 = state.code; reverse
f000 = state.sname;
end
```

With this example the code field is displayed in reverse video when the form is displayed. One or more of the attributes described in the following sections can be combined for use with any single screen field.

Autonext

When data is input from a form, the user presses the Enter key to complete the entry of data into a named field. Pressing the Enter key moves the cursor to the next field listed in the input statement.

The autonext attribute moves the cursor automatically to the next field without the user pressing the Enter key. When the autonext attribute is used, the cursor is automatically moved to the next field when the end of the current field is reached. The Enter key may also still be used to move to the next field.

Comments

The comments attribute associates a comment with a screen field. When the field is active, that is the cursor is displayed in the field, the comment is displayed.

```
attributes
a0 = state.code;
f000 = state.sname, comments = "Please enter a
state name"
```

When a form is displayed, one line of the screen is reserved as a location where comments are displayed. The default position where comments are displayed is line 23. This can be changed with the options statement.

```
options
  comment line 4
```

Downshift

The downshift attribute shifts any upper-case letters entered by the user to lower-case letters before they are passed to the input statement. Even though the user may type an upper-case letter, it will be shifted to lower case before being stored in the variable listed in the input statement.

Format

The format attribute controls the display of a a variable of type decimal, smallfloat, float or date.

For `decimal`, `smallfloat` or `float` type variables, a format string of pound signs (#) is used to show how the number is displayed.

```
attributes
f000 = table.attribute, format = "###.##"
```

Any program variable displayed to this form field will be shown with three digits before the decimal point, a decimal point, and two decimal digits, `999.99`.

If the value to be displayed is shorter than the field, the number is right-justified and padded with leading blanks. If the number is wider than the format string, but the field is wide enough to display the number, the number is displayed and a warning will be given. As with any field, a variable value that is too wide to fit in the form field will cause a program error. Numbers will be rounded to fit within the format specified.

The following symbols are used in the format string to affect the display of a variable of type `date`

format string	usage
mm	two letter abbreviation of the month
mmm	three letter abbreviation of the month
dd	two place abbreviation of the day
ddd	three letter abbreviation of the day
yy	two digit year
yyy	three digit year

```
attributes
a1 = table.field, format =  "mmmdddyyy";
```

This will display the date as `SunJany89`. Spaces can be used in the format specification. For example, the format `mmm ddd yyy` will display the same date as `Sun Jan y89`. Any other characters will be displayed too. For example the format `mmm-ddd-yyy` will cause the same date to be displayed as `Sun-Jan-y89`.

Include

The `include` attribute lists acceptable values for field entry to a field.

```
attributes
f001 = table.field, include = (1,2,3,4);
```

This example will allow the values 1, 2, 3 and 4 to be entered into the screen field. An attempt to enter any other value will cause an error message to be displayed. A range of values can also be given.

```
attributes
f001 = table.field, include = (1 to 4);
```

Noentry

The `noentry` attribute prevents data from being entered into a screen field.

Picture

The `picture` attribute provides a pattern for data typed into a field.

```
attributes
f001 = table.field, picture = "##-##-###-###"
```

When accessed from an input statement, this field will display as [- - -   ], including the delimiters. Each pound sign in the picture indicates a place where a digit can be entered into the field.

A digit can be entered into the field anywhere that a pound sign appears in the picture. If the user types anything other than a digit, the character will be ignored and the cursor will stay at the same position. The literal characters, the three minus signs, are skipped over as characters are entered by the user.

All the characters in the field, the digits typed by the user and the literals shown in the picture are saved into the variable named in the input statement. For example, the variable might hold the value 12-12-123x123 after the user input.

In addition to the pound sign, two other characters can be used in the picture. An upper case A indicates a position where a letter is to be entered into the field. An upper-case X indicates a position where any character, letter, digit or special character can be entered into the field.

```
f1  =  table.field, picture = "AA####.AA(XX)"
```

This field will be displayed as [. ( )]. The user can type any letter into the first two positions of the field, any digit into the next four positions of the field, any two letters in the next two positions and any character in the last two positions.

Required

The required attribute forces the entry of data into the specified field. If no data is entered into the field, and attempt to leave the field will cause an error message to be displayed.

If both a required and a default attribute are associated with a field, the default value will be used to satisfy the required attribute.

Reverse

The reverse attribute causes the selected field to be displayed in reverse video.

Upshift

The upshift attribute will cause any lower case characters entered into a field by the user to be shifted to upper case.

Verify

With the `verify` attribute, the user must enter data into a field twice before the data is accepted. This attribute is used to help assure that data is entered correctly by the user.

DEFAULTS AND WITHOUT DEFAULTS

Default values can be assigned to screen fields by using the `default` attribute in a form specification.

```
attributes
a0 = state.code, default = "CA";
f000 = state.sname, default = "California"
```

When this form is accessed from a running program with an `input` statement, the default values listed in the form specification are shown on screen. If the user does not change the default value shown for a field, that value is left in the variable for that field listed in the `input` statement.

Note that the default values for the form are displayed when the form is accessed by an `input` statement, not when the form is first displayed with a `display form` statement.

The `without defaults` clause of the input statement will override the default values specified in th attributes section of a screen form. program where the values of the program variables have been preassigned the values NV and Nevada

```
database stores
main
  define
    code like state.code,
    sname like state.sname,
    msg char(20)
  open form state from "state"
  display form state
```

```
      let state = "Nevada"
      let code = "NV"
      let msg = "A test message"
      display by name without defaults code,sname
      sleep 10
      clear screen
end main
```

Assume the following attributes in the form specification

```
attributes
a0 = state.code, default = "CA";
f000 = state.sname, default = "California"
```

When this program is run, NV and Nevada will appear on screen instead of the default values found in the form specification, CA and California. If the program variables contain null values, the screen fields will be blank when the program is run and the form is displayed.

The without defaults statement causes the values held in the program variables listed by the input statement to be used. Any default values listed in the form specification are ignored. To have the contents of program variables display on the screen-form, the without defaults statement must be used.

BEFORE AND AFTER FIELD

The input statement has two optional clauses, before field and after field. Statements associated with the before clause are executed before the cursor enters a screen field. Statement associated with the after clause are executed as the cursor exits the field.

```
database stores
main
   define
     code like state.code,
```

```
      sname like state.sname,
      m_text char(30)
    open form state from "state"
    display form state
    input by name sname, code
      before field sname
        let m_text = "Entering Field sname"
        message m_text
      after field sname
        let m_test = "Leaving field sname"
        message m_text
        let m_text = null
    end input
    sleep 2
    close form state
    clear screen
  end main
```

Note that an end input statement has been added to show the end of the input statement. This optional end statement is needed as the input statement becomes more complex.

The two statements after the before field sname clause will be executed before the cursor enters the field sname. The three statements associated with the after field clause are executed as the cursor leaves the sname field.

SCREEN ARRAYS

A query can select multiple tuples from a relation. These multiple tuples can then be copied into a program array, one tuple per array element.

A screen form can include a screen array. This screen array can be used to display some of the tuples held in a program array. The program array is automatically linked to the screen array with the display array or input array statement as shown in the next sections.

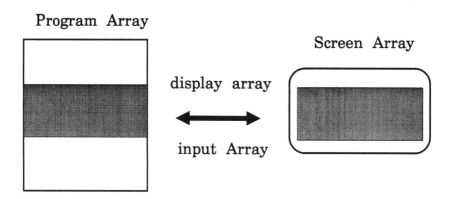

A portion of the tuples held in the program array can be displayed to the screen array at any one time. For example, if the program array holds 200 tuples, and the screen array has ten elements, ten tuples held in the program array can be displayed on the screen array at any one time.

of a screen form containing a screen array. The screen array is defined in the instructions portion of the screen form and is named s_array

```
database stores
screen
{
    code                State Name
    [a0]                [f000                       ]
    [a0]                [f000                       ]
    [a0]                [f000                       ]
    [a0]                [f000                       ]
```

```
        [a0]               [f000                    ]
        [a0]               [f000                    ]
        [a0]               [f000                    ]
        [a0]               [f000                    ]
        [a0]               [f000                    ]
        [a0]               [f000                    ]
}
tables
state
attributes
a0 = state.code;
f000 = state.sname;
instructions
screen record s_rec[15] ( state.* )
end
```

In this example the screen array is ten elements long. There are
ten rows in the screen section, one for each array element. Note
that there are multiple copies of the fields, one copy for each screen
array element.

THE DISPLAY ARRAY STATEMENT

The display array statement creates the linkage between the
program array and a screen array automatically.

```
database stores
main
  define
    c_rec array[100] of record
      code char(2),
      sname char(15)
    end record,
    pointer smallint
  declare c_state cursor for
    select * from state order by code
  let pointer = 1
```

```
   foreach c_state into c_rec[pointer].*
     let pointer = pointer + 1
   end foreach
   let pointer = pointer -1
   if pointer > 1 then
     open form state from "state"
     call set_count(pointer)
     display form state
     message "number of records found ", pointer
     display array c_rec to s_rec.*
   else
     message "No Records to display"
     sleep 1
   end if
end main
```

The active set of tuples retrieved by the query is left in the array c_rec by the foreach statement. If records are found in the database, they are displayed by the display array statement.

SETCOUNT( )

Note the call to the built-in function setcount in the example program above. This built-in function must be called before any display array or input array statement. This call allows the display array or input array statement to know how many elements of the program array contain data.

This function must be called with the number of data elements available in the program array before any display statements. If you don't make this call, the program will run, but no data will be displayed.

MOVING DATA ON THE SCREEN

When the sample program shown above is run, it finds 50 records, one for each state. The program will display the first ten records held in the program array to the screen array. The cursor keys can be used to move the cursor from one row of the screen array to the next, either up or down.

The display array statement automatically moves the data found in the program array up and down within the screen form as cursor keys are pressed. For example, when the cursor is moved to the last line of the screen array with the down-cursor key, and the down-cursor key is pressed again, the data displayed on screen will all be moved up one row and the next row of data available in the program array will appear on the last line of the screen array.

If the cursor is moved to the top line of the screen form, and the up-cursor key is pressed again, all the data will be moved down a line and the first record of the program array will re-appear on the first line of the screen form.

The cursor keys can be used in this fashion to move all the records found in the program array up and down within the screen array. An attempt to move to far in either direction, past the last tuple available in the program array, will generate an error message.

On terminals which have function keys, the f3 function key will scroll the displayed data up on screen to show the next available page of data. Similarly, the f4 function key will scroll the displayed data to the previous page of data held in the program array.

STOP DISPLAYING DATA

The escape key (esc on many terminals) will stop the display of data to the screen by the display array statement. The interrupt character or quit character will also stop the display of data. The quit or interrupt may also, of course, immediately stop the running program.

The sequence of keystrokes that generate an interrupt signal varies from system to system. It is often the key marked del or is produced by holding down the control key and pressing c. The Consult your system documentation or your system administrator to find how to issue an interrupt. Interrupt and quit signals, and the method of servicing them, are discussed in chapter 12.

THE ON KEY CLAUSE

An on-key clause can be added to the display array statement to allow certain key sequences to have an immediate effect while the display array statement is running. , note the addition of the end display statement

```
display array c_rec to s_rec.*
  on key (control-i)
    message "control-i was typed"
    sleep 1
    message " "
end display
```

This statement will display the contents of the program array c_rec to the screen record s_rec, just as in the prior example. In addition, as long as the display array statement is executing, typing a control-i by holding down the control key and pressing i will have the immediate effect of displaying the message control-i was pressed. Any key can be used to similar effect, for example on key (A).

THE INPUT ARRAY STATEMENT

The input array statement displays the values held in a program array to a screen array. In addition, the input array statement allows the user to make changes to the data displayed on screen.

```
database stores
main
  define
    c_rec array[100] of record
      code char(2),
      sname char(15)
    end record,
    pointer smallint
  declare c_state cursor for
    select * from state order by code
  let pointer = 1
  foreach c_state into c_rec[pointer].*
    let pointer = pointer + 1
  end foreach
  let pointer = pointer -1
  if pointer > 1 then
    open form state from "state"
    call set_count(pointer)
    display form state
    message "number of records found: ", pointer
    input array c_rec without defaults
      from s_rec.*
  else
    message "No Records to display"
    sleep 1
  end if
end main
```

This program will display the data held in the program array to the specified screen array. Note the without defaults clause of the input array statement. If this clause were missing, none of the values held in the program array would be displayed on the screen.

The function keys and cursor control keys described in the display array statement are all available for moving the program data within the screen array. The input array statement can also be stopped with an escape or by typing the key sequences for the interrupt or quit signal.

The display array statement only displayed data to the screen form. With the input array statement, the user can change the data as it appears on screen. New rows of data can be added, rows of data can be removed, and the data in existing rows can be changed. Each of these operations is shown in following sections

Before and After Field

The input array statement has a before field and after field clause. They have the same effect as the before field and after field clauses in the display array statement. These clauses allow a group of statements to be executed before the cursor enters a screen field, or after the cursor leaves a screen field.

On-Key

The function of the on-key clause is described at length in the above section about the on-key clause of the display array statement.

Before and After Row

The before row clause can execute one or more statements before the cursor is moved into a new row. The after row clause can execute one or more statements as the cursor leaves the current row.

```
input array c_rec without defaults from s_rec.*
  before row
    message "A new row has been entered"
  after row
    message "Leaving the row"
end input
```

Changing Data in a Screen Row

The user can type new information over the information displayed
in a field on thescreen. If the information on-screen is changed,
the information held in the database must also be changed. There
are a variety of ways to accomplish this, here is a sample of one
method

```
database stores
main
  define
    r_state array[100] of record like state.*,
    r_before record like state.*,
    pointer, p_rec smallint
  declare c_state cursor for
    select * from state order by code
  let pointer = 1
  let r_before.code = null
  let r_before.sname = null
  foreach c_state into r_state[pointer].*
    let pointer = pointer + 1
  end foreach
  let pointer = pointer -1
  call set_count(pointer)
  open form state from "state"
  display form state
  if pointer < 1 then
    message "The table is empty"
  else
    message "Records Found ", pointer
  end if
```

```
    input array r_state without defaults
      from s_rec.*
      before row
        let p_rec = arr_curr()
        let r_before.code = r_state[p_rec].code
        let r_before.state = r_state[p_rec].state
      after row
        if r_before.code <> r_state[p_rec].code or
           r_before.sname <> r_state[p_rec].sname
           then
          update state set
            code = r_state[p_rec].code,
            sname = r_state[p_rec].sname
            where state.code = r_before.code
          message "Record Updated"
        end if
    end input
end main
```

When a row is first entered, the contents of the row are saved into the record r_before with the statements listed with the before_row clause. Later, when the cursor moves off the row the contents of the row before it was entered and after it was left are compared. If they are different, the database is updated.

The input array statement keeps the program array and the screen array synchronized. Any changes made to the screen array are also made to the program array.

Note the call to the function arr_curr(). The cursor can be moved with the cursor keys or function keys. The function arr_curr returns the row of the program array that is currently in-use. The function arr_count() returns the number of program array elements that are currently in-use. There is another function scr_line() which returns the number of the screen row that is currently in use.

Program array

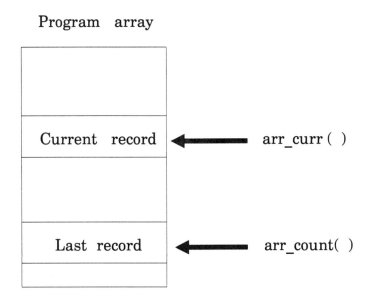

As the cursor is moved from row to row, the value returned by arr_curr() will point to the currently selected program array element and the value returned by scr_line() will be the number of the screen array element the cursor is currently pointing to.
Before and after Delete

The before delete clause will execute a group of statements just before a row is deleted from the screen. The after delete clause will execute one or more statements just after a screen row is deleted.

On most systems, the F1 key will delete the current screen row. This can be changed with the options statement

```
options
  delete key control-u
```

This statement will change the key sequence used to delete a screen row. After this statement is executed, a row is deleted by holding the `control` key and pressing o. Certain keys are not available because the are permanently reserved for other uses. They are

```
control-a
control-d
control-r
control-l
control-b
control-x
```

Before and After Insert

This example adds a `before insert`, `after insert`, and options statement. It assigns the `insert` key as `control-i`

```
database stores
main
  define
    r_state array[100] of record like state.*
    r_before record like state.*
    pointer, p_rec, new_row smallint
  options
    insert key control-i,
    delete key control-o
  declare c_state cursor for
    select * from state order by code
  let pointer = 1
  let r_before.code = null
  let r_before.sname = null
  foreach c_state into r_state[pointer].*
    let pointer = pointer + 1
  end foreach
  let pointer = pointer -1
  call set_count
  open form state from "state"
```

```
display form state
if pointer < 1 then
  message "The table is empty"
else
  message "Records Found ", pointer
end if
input array r_state without defaults
  from s_rec.*
  before row
    let p_rec = arr_curr()
    let r_before.code = r_state[p_rec].code
    let r_before.state = r_state[p_rec].state
  after row
    if r_before.code <> r_state[p_rec].code or
       r_before.sname <> r_state[p_rec].sname
       then
      if not new_row then
        update state set
          code = r_state[p_rec].code,
          sname = r_state[p_rec].sname
          where state.code = r_before.code
        message "Record Updated"
      end if
    end if
    before insert
      let new_row = true
    after insert
      if r_state[p_rec].code is not null and
         r_state[p_rec].sname is not null then
        insert into state
          values (r_state[p_rec].*)
      end if
      let new_row = false
    after delete
      delete from state
        where state.code = r_before.code
  end input
end main
```

This program will insert a new row into the database whenever a new row is inserted on-screen. Note the addition of the flag new_row. This flag is used to assure that an insert of a new row will not be followed directly by an attempted update.

This program is not complete. There are no checks against inserting a duplicate row into the database for example. Tailoring the input array statement to the needs of your specific application can be difficult. Using the input array statement well can be very demanding.

Next Field

During the execution of the input array statement, the cursor can be moved from field to field with the tab key, the Enter key, or the cursor keys. The Enter key and tab keys will move the cursor from one field to the other in the order those fields are named in the attributes section of the screen form definition. This ordering can be changed with the next field clause.

```
after field ex11
  if r_scr is null then
    next field ex12
  end if
```

Exit Input

An input array statement can be ended, and control passed to the next statement following the end input statement with the exit input clause.

```
input array r_state without defaults from s_rec.*
  after field code
    if r_state[p_rec].code = "XX" then
      exit input
    end if
end input
```

Execution Order of Clauses

The various clauses of the input array statement are executed in this order of precedence

```
before row
before insert or delete
before field
on key
after field
after insert or delete
after row
after input
```

OTHER SCREEN CONTROL

There are other ways that a screen form can be controlled.

Refresh The Screen

The entire contents of the screen can be re-drawn at any time by holding down the control key and pressing r for re-draw.

Delete a Field

During the execution of an input array or input statement used with a screen form, the field that the cursor is currently in can be emptied by typing control-r.

QUERY BY EXAMPLE

The user can enter search criteria for a query into the fields of a screen form. The information the user enters into the screen fields is used to qualify the where clause of a select statement.

```
database stores
main
  define
    s_query, query char(512),
    r_tbl array [100] or record like state.*,
    c_recs smallint
  defer interrupt
  open form state from "state"
  display form state
  clear form
  intialize s_query, query to null
  let int_flag = 0
  construct s_query
    on code, sname
    from code, sname
  let query = "select * from state
    where", s_query clipped,
    "order by code"
  prepare p_query from query
  declare c_tbl scroll cursor for p_query
  let c_recs = 1
  let int_flag = 0
  foreach c_tbl into r_tbl[c_recs].*
    let c_recs = c_recs + 1
  end foreach
  let c_recs = c_recs - 1
  if int_flag <> 0 then
    message "Interrupt - no records selected"
    let int_flag = 0
    exit program
  else
    call set_count(c_recs)
    display array r_tbl to s_rec.*
  end if
end main
```

When this program is run, the screen form appears. The cursor is left in the first screen field. The user can enter qualifications for the search into these fields, one at a time. The entry of search qualifications is ended by pressing the escape key. If the user presses the escape key without entering any search restrictions, all the records in the relation will be selected.

For example, the user could type CA into the first screen field. When the program continues, the database will be searched for records where state.code is equal to CA. Any valid boolean expression which can be used as part of the where clause in a select statement can be entered into the screen field by the user.

Here is how the program works. First, the query is constructed into the character variable s_query. The statement

```
construct s_query on code,sname from code, sname
```

allows the user to enter values into the form fields on screen, one-at-a-time. The information entered by the user will be used to form a where clause in a select statement. The information entered by the user is combined with the rest of a full select statement in the next statement let query = "select * from.

This creates an image of a select statement which is held in the character variable query. This select statement must be prepared before it can be executed. The next statement does this preparation. Note that the name of the prepared query, in this case p_query does not have to be declared in the define section of the program

```
        prepare p_query from query
```

The next statement attaches the prepared query to a cursor

```
        declare c_tbl scroll cursor for p_query
```

This cursor can now be used to select an active set of tuples from a relation.

WINDOWS

A new window can be opened on screen with the window statement.

```
open window w_status at 2, 34
  with 1 rows 10 columns
  attribute (reverse, border)
display searching at 1,1
let c_recs = 1
let int_flag = 0
foreach c_tbl into r_tbl[c_recs].*
  let c_recs = c_recs + 1
end foreach
let  c_recs = c_recs - 1
close window w_status
```

These statements, when added to the previous program, will cause
a separate window to appear on screen at row two, column 34. This
window is one row high and ten columns wide. The message
Searching is displayed in this window. When the database has
been searched, the window is erased form the screen.

The window is placed over the information that is already on-
screen. When the window is erased, the information that was
under the window is still there and reappears.

The attributes for a window can be

border   to draw a border around the window

color   white, yellow, magenta, red, cyan, blue, black

reverse   show the window in reverse video

The prompt line, message line, comment line and form line can
also be set for the window with attributes

```
form line 1
prompt line 2
message line 3
comment line 4
```

Anything can be displayed in a separate window: data, forms or
menus.

14

Reports

This chapter describes how reports are written with a 4GL program. Data is collected by a 4GL program. This data can be extracted from a database or computed by the running program. The collected data is sent to a report routine for printing in a suitable format.

Writing reports with the report writer is easy. The Informix-4GL report writer is superb.

COLLECTING DATA FOR A REPORT

Here is a sample report program. It is the Informix supplied demo program report1.4gl

```
database stores
main
  define p_customer record like customer.*
  declare q_curs cursor for
  select * from
  start report cust_list
  foreach q_curs into p_customer.*
    output to report cust_list (p_customer.*)
  end foreach
  finish report cust_list
end main
report cust_list(r_customer)
```

246

```
    define r_customer record like customer.*
    format every row
end report
```

This program prints a report with one group of data for each record retrieved from the database. The report is started with the start report cust_list statement. The report is ended with the statement finish report. The main program selects all the tuples from the customer relation. Each of the tuples are sent to the report for printing on at a time.

The printed report will have one line for each tuple sent to the report. The report will be divided into pages automatically. This automatic formatting of the report into pages shows some of the convenience of the report writer. The report writer provides many powerful automatic features as described below.

The call to the report program is issued with the statement output to report. Do not use the call statement to access a report. While the program will compile, it will not run correctly.

REPORT FORMAT

The report writer has assumptions about the format of printed reports built-in. These assumptions are used when printing data. The report writer assumes that the printed page is a certain length with a fixed upper, lower, left and right-hand margin. This is shown in the next illustration.

The page format can be changed in the output section of a report routine.

```
database stores
main
  define p_customer record like customer.*
  declare q_curs cursor for
  select * from
  start report cust_list
  foreach q_curs into p_customer.*
    output to report cust_list (p_customer.*)
  end foreach
  finish report cust_list
end main
report cust_list(r_customer)
  define r_customer record like customer.*
  output
    left margin 4
    right margin 4
    top margin 4
    bottom margin 4
    page length 24
  format every row
end report
```

The data printed on a report falls between pre-set margins. The values for the margins and page length are given as integers. Lengths are in lines, widths are in character positions. Values can be set to zero to eliminate a specific margin.

Margins

The left margin is automatically set to a width of five spaces until changed by a left margin statement. This determines where the beginning of an output line will appear on the output page.

The right margin is at column 132 until changed with a right margin statement.

The top and bottom margins are set to three lines each until changed with a top margin or bottom margin statement.

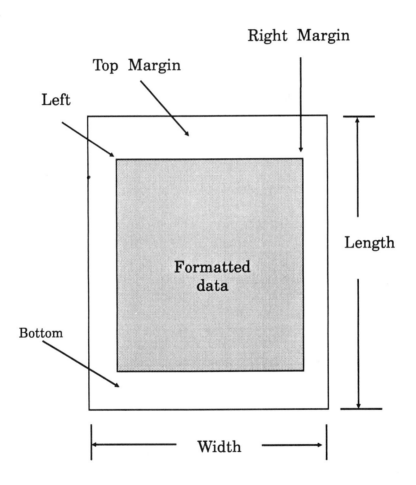

Page Length

The page length is set to 66 lines by default. It can be changed with
the page length statement. The page length must be set long
enough to allow the top and bottom margins and at least one line
of output data to be printed.

DIRECTING THE REPORT TO A FILE

A report is written to the screen until the destination is changed
with the report to statement in the options section of the report
routine.

```
output
   report to "label.out"
```

This same mechanism can be used with some operating systems
to direct the output of a report to a specific device like a printer.
For example this might direct the output of a report to a printer
when using the UNIX operating system

```
output
report to "/dev/printer/lpr"
```

Contact your system administrator or system documentation to
find out the name of the file associated with a printer for your
particular system.

The start report statement can also be used to redirect the
output of a report to a printer or file. Below are three examples

```
start report r_name to "filename"
start report r_name to file_name
start report r_name to printer
```

The report to statement in the output section of a report will only accept a literal value for a destination name. It will not accept a variable as a value. The to file_name clause of the start report statement will accept a character variable.

```
database stores
main
  define
    p_customer record like customer.*,
    destination char(20)
  declare q_curs cursor for
  select * from
  let destination = "/dev/null"
  start report cust_list to destination
```

When using the UNIX operating system, printer output will be directed to the file named either lp or lpr, depending on your system. See your system administrator to find out which is in use on your system. When running with the DOS operating system, printer output will be automatically directed to lpt1.

ORDERING DATA FOR THE REPORT

A program sends tuples to a report routine on at a time. The report prints the tuples in the order received. If the tuples are sent to the report in a different order, the reported data will be printed in a different order. Thus, one way to order a report is to have the program that compiles the data order that data before sending it to the report program.

The order by clause of a select statement can also order data for a report. of a report program that will order the data sent to it by the calling program

```
start report cust_list
foreach q_curs into p_customer.*
  output to report cust_list (p_customer.*)
end foreach
```

```
finish report cust_list
. . .
report cust_list(r_customer)
  define r_customer record like customer.*
  order by r_customer.zipcode
  format every row
end report
```

This program will produce a report where the printed information is in zip-code order. Note that there is no provision for ordering data in descending order with the order by statement.

PRESENTING DATA

The format section of a report can include statements to create page headings and footings. This section of a report routine can include statements to format output data in any manner you specify. Finally, statements in the format section of a report can be used to group data or perform calculations like averages and totals. Each of these operations is described in the following sections of this chapter.

GROUPS OF DATA

Groups of data can be manipulated with data control blocks in the format section of a a report. Each row of data sent by a calling program can be processed with the every row and on every row control blocks as described below.

Each page can have a header or trailer printed with the page header and page trailer statements. The first page of a report can have a unique header with the first page header statement.

Data groups are based on the values of a particular attribute. For example, the tuples from the customer relation in the stores database could be grouped by zip code. Operations can be performed before or after each group of data.

EVERY ROW

Every row of data passed to a report routine is printed with a default format when the every row clause is used in the format section of a report routine. The simplest case was shown in the previous sample program

```
report cust_list(r_customer)
  define r_customer record like customer.*
  order by r_customer.zipcode
  format
    every row
end report
```

ON EVERY ROW

Every row of data passed to a report routine can be processed with statements associated with the on every row control block.

```
report cust_list(r_customer)
  define r_customer record like customer.*
  order by r_customer.zipcode
  format
    on every row
      print r_customer.company, r_customer.zipcode
end report
```

This report routine will print the company name and zip-code to the screen for every tuple it receives. The print statement is described at length in the next section.

THE PRINT STATEMENT

The display statement, described in Chapter 13, formats data for display on-screen. Similarly, the print statement formats rows of data printed in a report.

```
report cust_list(r_customer)
  define r_customer record like customer.*
  order by r_customer.zipcode
  format
    on every row
      print
        r_customer.company, 3 spaces,
        r_customer.zipcode
end report
```

The print statement can use all the same formatting operations that are available to the display statement. For example, character strings can be clipped or concatenated and numbers can be displayed with a selected format.

```
on every row
  print
    r_customer.customer_num using "cnum: ####",
    4 spaces,
    r_customer.company, 3 spaces,
    r_customer.phone, 4 spaces,
    r_customer.zipcode
```

SPACES AND COLUMN POSITIONS

In addition to the operations available with the display statement, the print statement can print data at a certain column position or skip spaces.

```
on every row
  print
    column 1, r_customer.customer_num,
    4 spaces, r_customer.company,
    column 20, r_customer.phone,
    1 space, r_customer.zipcode
```

Note that either the word space or spaces can be used.

Printing can be moved to a specified column with the column keyword. It is better to use the column notation instead of the spaces clause or a literal string of spaces like "   "

Each print statement will cause a new line of data to be printed. Ending a print statement with a semicolon will suppress the next line and cause printing to continue on the current line.

```
on every row
  print column 1, r_customer.customer_num;
  print 4 spaces, r_customer.company;
  print column 20, r_customer.phone;
  print 1 space, r_customer.zipcode
```

This statement will print the same results as shown in the previous example.

SKIP LINES

The skip lines statement can be used to skip one or more lines during report printing.

```
on every row
  print column 1, r_customer.customer_num;
  print 4 spaces, r_customer.company;
  print column 20, r_customer.phone;
  print 1 space, r_customer.zipcode
  skip 1 line
```

This statement causes the report to be double spaced. The skip statement can be written as skip 1 line or skip 10 lines.

NEED LINES

The need lines statement assures that there are enough lines left on the current page to print the next group of data entirely on that page.

```
on every row
  need 2 lines
  print
    column 1, r_customer.customer_num,
    4 spaces, r_customer.company,
    column 20, r_customer.phone,
    1 space, r_customer.zipcode
```

The need 2 lines statement used in this example will assure that each group of data, a print line and a blank line, will appear on the same page.

PAGE HEADERS AND TRAILERS

Page header control blocks can contain statements which are executed when the top of every page is encountered. The first page header control block can contain statements executed at the first page of the report. The page trailer control block can contain statements that are executed when the end of any page is reached.

```
format
  on every row
    need 2 lines
    print
      column 1, r_customer.customer_num,
      4 spaces, r_customer.company,
```

```
      column 20, r_customer.phone,
      1 space, r_customer.zipcode
    skip 1 line
  first page header
    print column 20 "Company Phone Report"
  page header
    skip 1 line
    print column 20, "Company Phone Report-Cont'd"
  page trailer
    skip 1 line
    print column 10, "——————————"
```

This program will print an individual message on the top of the first page. Each following page will have the message in the page header control block at the top.

Each page will have the last line message printed on the bottom.

LAST ROW

Statements in the on last row control block are executed when the last tuple is encountered.

```
format
  on last row
    print "Last row found!"
```

SKIP TO TOP OF PAGE

Printing can be forced to the top of the next page with the skip to top of page statement.

```
on every row
  print column 1, r_customer.customer_num;
  print 4 spaces, r_customer.company;
  print column 20, r_customer.phone;
  print 1 space, r_customer.zipcode
  skip to top of page
```

This example will print one tuple per page.

PAUSE

Output directed to the screen can be paused at the end of each page with the pause statement. The pause statement has no effect when report output is directed to a file or the printer.

```
page trailer
  pause "Press ENTER to continue printing"
```

GROUPS OF DATA

The before group of and after group of control blocks contain statements that are executed when a certain variable changes value.

```
format
  on every row
    print
      column 1, r_customer.customer_num,
      4 spaces, r_customer.company,
      column 20, r_customer.phone
    skip 1 line
  before group of r_customer.zipcode
    need 4 lines
    print "Zipcode: ", r_customer.zipcode
  after group of r_customer.zipcode
    print "————"
```

```
first page header
   print column 20 "Company Phone Report"
page header
   skip 1 line
   print column 20, "Company Phone Report-Cont'd"
page trailer
   skip 1 line
   print column 10, "————————"
```

This program will print the zip-code and a short message whenever the value of zipcode changes. Note that the tuples are ordered by the calling program. This report assumes that the tuples are sent in order of zip-code.

Note the statement need four lines in the before group of control block. This assures that there is enough space remaining on the page to print the group header and at least two lines of data.

The skip to top of page statement can be used in the before group of statement or the after group of statement to start each new group at the top of a new page.

ADDITIONAL STATEMENTS

Additional 4GL statements can be added to a report inside a control block.

```
report cust_list ( r_customer )
   define r_customer record like customer.*,
   rec_count smallint
format
   on every row
      let rec_count = rec_count + 1
      need 2 lines
      print
         column 1, r_customer.customer_num,
         4 spaces, r_customer.company,
         column 20, r_customer.phone,
```

```
            1 space, r_customer.zipcode
          skip 1 line
      on last row
          if rec_count > 0 then
            print "Records Found: ", rec_count
          else
            print "No Records Reported"
          end if
      first page header
          let rec_count = 0
          print column 20 "Company Phone Report"
      page header
          skip 1 line
          print column 20, "Company Phone Report-Cont'd"
      page trailer
          skip 1 line
          print column 10, "_____"
  end report
```

Note that additional 4GL statements can only be added within a
control block. This is why the variable rec_count is initialized to
zero within the first page header control block.

REPORT ONLY VARIABLES

Several built-in variables are available in a report routine. These
variables can not be used in a main program or function. They are
only available within a report.

Lineno

The lineno variable contains the number of the line that is
currently being printed.

```
        print column 10, lineno using "Line <<<"
```

Pageno

The pageno variable contains the current page number of the printed report.

```
page trailer
   print pageno using "page <<<<"
```

Time

The built-in variable time contains the current value of the system clock. The time is held as a string in the format HH:MM:SS.

```
page header
  print column 1, time
```

BUILT IN FUNCTIONS

Many, but not all, built-in functions can be called from within a control block of a report routine. These functions are listed in the Report section of the Informix supplied reference manual.

Built-in aggregate functions are also described in this section. These aggregate functions behave differently than the aggregate functions used with the select statement. They are count, percent, average, max and min.

The built-in functions are where we leave our discussion of the Informix-4GL language and you start your own adventure. Good luck and good programming!

Appendix A

Reserved Words

These identifiers are all reserved for use by Informix-4gl. They should not be used as names for identifiers, functions, reports, or labels:

absolute	array	begin
accept	as	between
add	asc	blink
after	ascii	blue
all	at	bold
allowing	attribute	border
alter	attributes	botton
and	audit	break
any	auto	by
arg_val	average	call
arr_count	avg	case
arr_curr	before	char

check	database	downshift
clear	date	drop
clipped	day	else
close	dba	end
cluster	decimal	entry
column	declare	err_get
columns	defaults	err_print
command	defer	err_quite
comment	define	error
commit	delete	errorlog
composites	delimiter	esc
connect	desc	escape
construct	describe	every
continue	defaults	exclusive
control	dim	execute
correct	display	exists
count	displayonly	exit
create	distinct	exitnow
current	dos	external
cursor	double	false
cyan	down	fetch

field	in	lineno
file	include	lines
finish	incorrect	lock
first	index	log
float	initialize	long
flush	input	magenta
for	insert	main
foreach	instructions	margin
form	integer	master
form4gl	interrupt	matches
format	into	max
from	invisible	mdy
function	is	menu
globals	joining	message
grant	key	min
green	label	mode
group	last	modify
having	let	money
headings	level	month
help	like	name
if	line	need

noentry	startlog	underline
netauf	statistics	unique
next	step	unix
nextfield	stop	unload
no	sum	unlock
normal	synonym	up
not	systables	update
notfound	table	upshift
noupdate	tables	user
null	temp	using
num_args	then	validata
of	through	value
on	thru	values
open	time	verify
options	to	view
spaces	today	wait
sqlawarn	top	waiting
sqlca	trailer	warning
sqlcode	true	weekday
sqlerrd	type	when
start	typedef	whenever

where	window	year
while	without	yellow
white	work	zerofill
with	wrap	

Appendix B

Functions

Here is a listing of the built-in functions for Informix-4gl. See the Informix supplied documentation for a more complete description of each of these functions.

arr_curr(variable)

Used with screen arrays. Returns the number of the current progam array row.

arr_count(variable)

Ues with screen arrays. Returns the number of rows currently stored in a program array.

ascii numeric-expression

Returns the single ascii character specified by the numeric expression.

character-expression clipped

removes trailing blanks from the character expression

column integer-number

Returns a string of blanks integer-number long.

date

Returns a date as a character string in the format "Thu Sep 2 1986"

date()

Converts a character string to date format. For example

```
end_date = date("12/13/1989")
```

day()

Accepts a date, returns the day of the month.

MDY(expression1,expression2,expression3)

Accepts three expressions which evaluate to integers. Returns a value of type date.

month(date-expression)

Accepts an expression of type date. Returns an integer from 1 to 12 representing the month.

scr_line()

A screen array function. Returns the number of the screen row that the cursor is currently on.

set_count(expression)

A screen array function. Accepts the number of rows held in a program array, sets the initial value of arr_count(). This MUST be called before any attempt to display data to or accept data from a screen array.

numeric-expression SPACES

returns a string numeric-expression characters long of spaces.

today

Returns todays date as supplied by the local operating system.

expression_1 USING expression_2

See the using statement in the text. The using function formats a character string held in expression one using the formatting information found in expression two.

      &   zero fills blank character positions

      #   maximum field width, doesn't change blanks

      *****   prints leading asterisks

      <   left-justifies numbers in field

      ,   literal-displays a comma

      .   literal-displays a period

      +   literal-displays a plus sign

      (literal-displays a left paren

)   literal-displays a right paren

      $ literal-displays a dollar sign

weekday(date=expression)

Accepts a date expression. Returns an integer from 0 to six where Sunday is 1, Monday is 2, and so on.

year(date_expression)

Accepts a data expression. Returns an integer representing the year.

Index

ORDER FORM

All the examples in this book are available on an IBM-PC format floppy disc. In addition, this disc contains a complete implementation of the Music database system. You will find this full of excellent examples of using Informix-4GL to construct a real system. For example, a complete demonstration of the input array statement is provided. A handy 4GL pocket-guide is also included with each order.

The floppy disc and handy pocket guide cost $21.50. There is a $2.50 charge for shipping and handling within the united states. There is a $8.50 charge for shipping outside the United States. To order, copy the form on the next page and send it along with your payment to

Paul Mahler
Sunday & Associates
1800 Market Street # 257
San Francsico, CA
94102
Telephone: 415-644-0440

Make checks payable to Paul Mahler. Allow two to four weeks for delivery. All payment must be in U.S. Dollars.

Name:

Telephone:

Company Name:

Shipping Address: Business Address:

Number of Copies: Cost:

                                    Shipping:

                                    Total Cost:

Method of Payment: check   visa   mastercard

Credit Card Number:

Expiration Date:

Signature:

For information on consulting, training, or
development services, circle here: Yes